WALKING WITH ANGELS

Journey Of Hope

BY MELVIN R. FRASS

Fairway Press
Lima, Ohio

WALKING WITH ANGELS

FIRST EDITION
Copyright © 1992 by
Melvin R. Frass

7948 / ISBN 1-55673-525-1   PRINTED IN U.S.A.

Dedicated
To all of the loved ones in my life
who have given me joy, comfort,
and happiness.

FOREWORD

The author acknowledges the use of several lines from the work of Edgar Allan Poe's historic and beautiful poem, *Annabelle Lee*, in passages of this manuscript. The name Rosalie is used in place of Annabelle Lee. The intent of the author is the expression of feeling by the characters in the story of Ralph and Rosalie.

All other quotations are correctly referenced in the script.

A special thanks to: St. Paul's Episcopal Church, Marion, Ohio, and Hughes Studio, Inc., John Rall, photographer, Marion, Ohio.

CHAPTER ONE

It was a beautiful autumn morning in the small Midwestern town of Vernon Heights. The sun shining through the tall oak and much smaller maple trees reflected the many changing colors of the season that was in transition. The tranquility of this miracle of nature seemed to be disturbed by the slowly moving funeral procession maneuvering through the town. The lead vehicle, a limousine, approached the entrance to Shady Pines cemetery and turned in. A hearse and a number of cars followed the limousine along the narrow roadway to where a tent had been set up and a grave prepared for interment. The procession stopped when it reached the burial site. Car doors opened and the family and friends of the deceased made their way to the grave site under the tent. As the coffin was removed from the hearse and carried and placed on the bier, it was apparent that there was a great deal of sorrow among those who were gathering under the tent. The mourning was for Rosalie Steele, a very dear lady, the dedicated mother of four children and the loving wife of Ralph Steele, the dean of technical education at the small business college located in Vernon Heights.

Rosalie and Ralph had moved to Vernon Heights two years earlier in order for him to accept the position as dean. It had apepared to be a successful career move, and a smooth one. All four of their children, Mark, Matthew, Eileen and Elicia, were married and had children.

When Rosalie became ill, it was a blow to the entire family since the children all lived in different places and could not be with their mother as much as they had wanted to be. She was the glue that kept everyone together and she took care of each one's needs. Now she was gone and she would be missed. At the service at the mortuary earlier, the Reverend John Harrigan, a Methodist minister, spoke of Rosalie as a devoted mother and wife, a firm supporter of her husband.

"They were a team complementing one another, and because of this very special relationship, theirs was a very special and true love," he said.

> *She was a child and I was a child*
> *In this kingdom by the sea*
> *But we loved with a love that*
> *was more than love.*

Reverend Harrigan continued, "We gather together as a people this morning to celebrate the earthly life and the eternal life of Rosalie Harter Steele. This morning, although our hearts are heavy and those of us who loved her will miss her a great deal, we also celebrate the fact that she has finished her course here on earth and has gone to be with God who we always know will claim his own — so we need not despair. We understand that the years of this life are numbered and our time, our turn, will also come when we return to be with the God who created us. It is an occasion of sorrow for ourselves, but it is an occasion of joy for Rosalie because she escapes the pain, the bonds, the limitations and death, all the kinds of difficulties that accompany frail and declining health.

We celebrate this morning her triumph over the grave and her entry into the kingdom of her Maker.

"She entered this life on the sixteenth day of July and was raised on a farm near Bayes, Ohio. And then on the twenty-eighth day of September in 1951, she married her life-long husband, Ralph, faithful companion of 36 years; love and devotion of a person who spent that time certainly enjoying those early years with her; certainly enjoying the creation and establishment of their home and their family; certainly sharing with her in the love and support and care of her parents; enjoying the good times that were; and of course, wrestling through the troubled waters until there was calm; the care he gave her during those last months, especially the last month. Rarely have I witnessed a man so devoted to his wife. Now into this marriage were born four children who are celebrating her life through their own lives.

"She was a devoted daughter, wife, and mother. Rosalie's life centered around her family and her home, always caring more for the well-being of her family than for herself. She was a very giving and loving person. In her own humble life she sought no recognition. Her greatest joy was simply loving her family — giving to them. She had a very deep faith that she confided in me, a faith she had long before she knew she was terminally ill. Rosalie was the kind of person who you enjoy being around, the kind of person who upon walking into a room, would light up the room. She possessed that magnetic, sparkling, giving personality that drew you to her.

"She was concerned with all those kinds of things that made a house a home. Her last goal was to build a nice new home in Vernon Heights — one that she selected from a house plan book. She designed the interior and even stained the woodwork. It was her creation — her dream, because of the joy that would follow sharing it with her children, her parents, and with her husband.

"Many things about Rosalie linger on, but the words giving, caring, sharing, working for you, being your advocate, stand out. Those are the kinds of things you remember this morning as you recall the years of her life. She was a great woman."

9

Everyone in the immediate family and close friends who were gathered for the final prayers over the casket did not notice the two men who were standing under a cluster of white maple trees a short distance away engaged in conversation. One of the men, an elderly distinguished looking man dressed in a black suit with a gray vest which matched the spats that partially covered his well polished black shoes, was speaking to a much younger man who was tall and handsome with dark wavy hair and wearing a navy blue suit. "Michael, as Ralph Steele's guardian angel, you will need to watch him closely at all times."

"Yes, Gordian," replied the young man.

"He's very emotionally disturbed now, and with our past experience with his accident, get in touch with me if you need help," the elderly man said as he brushed his white hair with his hand.

"I appreciate your kind offer of support. If the angel Joseph had not been with me, he may not have made it through the accident," replied Michael. He continued, "Having Joseph in the car holding Ralph when he passed out allowed me to steer the car away from the concrete embankment we just barely missed."

The Reverend Harrigan approached the casket which rested on the bier. He opened his prayer book and began to pray, ending with the intercession, "May she rest in peace."

CHAPTER TWO

Family and friends gathered for a luncheon held at the Methodist church basement in town, served by church members to accomodate those who were from out of town. The Steele family was grateful for this gesture because it relieved some tension in their time of grief. There was so much to talk about, the words were not there.

The children looked to their father for help. After all, he was the one to fix the broken bicycle or mend the torn doll. He was always there for their needs, so surely he would help them cope with the loss of their dear mother. Ralph tried to hold back the grief, the loss of a wife of 36 years, but could not keep his eyes dry of tears. He could not help this time — he was overtaken with the loss of Rosalie.

It was time to leave; Mark, Matthew, Eileen, and Elicia vowed to stay together — to communicate and visit even if they did live distances apart. "Let's try and get together for Christmas," suggested Mark, the eldest.

"And if we can't do that, we can always use the telephone," retorted Eileen. On the way out, Elicia grabbed her father's arm. "Dad, are you all right?" she asked. "Remember to take your medicine. Eileen and I both promised Mom that we would see to it that you did," she added.

"Yes I will sweetheart," replied Ralph, as he wrapped his arms around her. "Thanks for caring."

And so the Steele family went on their way, groping for a way to stay together like they used to, without the person who was the glue to keep them together.

CHAPTER THREE

Ralph returned to his office at the college the day after the funeral. He called his secretary, Violet Swanson, into his office and said, "Let's deal with any correspondence that has to be taken care of right away."

Violet always placed the mail on his desk. It was always in separate file folders designating mail that had to be answered, promotional literature from vendors, memos from the staff, and background material to be read. He motioned for her to sit down in one of the chairs beside his desk.

"Before we go over this," pointing to the file folders "how is my appointments calendar?" he asked.

"Everyone that I called to cancel an appointment understood and said they would wait until you returned," she replied, "except Mr. Sims. He wanted to see you as soon as you came in," she added.

Curtis Sims, an associate professor of applied technology was a friend. He and his wife, Maureen, attended social events with Rosalie and himself. The four were close friends.

"Get through this mail first," he said.

Violet Swanson was very thorough in going over all important items. She had come to work at the college a month after Ralph had accepted the position as dean. Her former job was at an insurance claims office which handled health and dental claims. A graduate of the business program at the college, she was married and had two children, both girls. Since one of the girls was beginning school and the other was in a day care program, the hours at the college worked out well. As she went through the mail, she explained the details for Ralph. He was then able to obtain sufficient information so he could respond to the items that needed attention.

"Violet, after you call Mr. Sims, please call those with whom we cancelled appointments and reschedule," he said with a smile. "It's business as usual," he added.

She smiled as she got up from the chair and said, "It's good to have you back. Many of us were concerned about you."

"Thank you Violet," he responded, and then added, "You were outstanding in covering for me and taking care of details."

"Thank you, Mr. Steele," she said. As she was leaving the room, she turned and said, "I'll call Mr. Sims to come down as soon as he can."

"Fine, Violet, fine" he replied.

It was a matter of minutes when Curtis Sims appeared in the doorway of Ralph's office, "Hi guy, may I come in?" he asked as he knocked on the doorframe.

"Sure, have a seat. What's on your mind?" Ralph queried in a businesslike tone.

"I just wanted to comfort you, old buddy," he said as he sat down in a chair directly in front of Ralph's desk. "Maureen and I," he continued, "we would like to be of some help. We thought you might like to have dinner with us tonight, since all of your kids have left and you're alone."

"Well thank you," replied Ralph. "That's very kind of you and Maureen."

"Then it's settled. We'll expect you around six o'clock," he said, then added, "I know you have a lot to catch up on around here, so I'll be on my way."

"Thanks Curtis, it's so thoughtful of Maureen and you. I'll see both of you at six," he said.

With that, Curtis and Ralph embraced as Curtis began to leave.

CHAPTER FOUR

The drive to Newman's Center, where Curtis and Maureen Sims lived, was thirty miles north on Highway 73. Ralph and Rosalie had been neighbors to the Sims' until the trustees at the college insisted that Ralph move to Vernon Heights. They believed that the dean of the college should have maximum exposure in the community.

As he was driving, he thought to himself — why her — why now? She was so devoted to her family, children, parents and to him. Why is her life less worthy when she was beginning to reach the golden years? How unfair, he surmised. As he turned west on Newman's Road, he remembered the days when he and Rosalie were neighbors to Maureen and Curtis Sims. He had been instrumental in obtaining a position for Curtis at the college when he was let go from another institution.

Ralph arrived at the Sims' house early. Maureen and Curtis were at the front door to greet him.

"I'm early folks, but I didn't expect so little traffic on the way up," he explained of his early arrival.

16

"And I thought you were just dying for my home cooking." Maureen's face blushed in embarrassment. She realized her poor choice of words.

"I'm sorry, I wasn't thinking," she said as she gestured with her arms for Ralph to come into the house. Curtis put his arm around Ralph and suggested that he sit down.

"Here's your favorite chair. Let's sit down and have a drink before we eat," he said.

"What would you like to drink, Ralph?" asked Maureen.

"A cola is fine," he answered.

"You always drank diet. Is that all right?" she asked.

"Sure," replied Ralph.

Maureen left the room and returned shortly with three drinks on a serving tray. She served the drinks, and joined Curtis and Ralph sitting down on the sofa. They talked about how the leaves on the trees in the woods that surrounded their house were turning color, displaying the beauty of the autumn season.

"It won't be long, Curtis, and you'll be picking up the leaves after they have fallen," Ralph said as he smiled.

"Yes it's work to rake the leaves, but I don't mind," Curtis replied.

Maureen excused herself saying, "If we're going to eat, I'd better check the oven."

Curtis began to talk, saying, "I didn't want to bring this up earlier, but while you were away several of the part time instructors dismissed their night classes early. It's caused some dissension among some of the full-time people."

"Did you do anything?" Ralph asked.

"No, I was waiting for you. I'd like to know how you'd want me to handle the situation," he replied.

"Well, let's talk about it first thing tomorrow morning," Ralph said.

"Dinner's on," Maureen yelled from the dining room.

"You guys will have to stop talking shop if you want to eat."

"We better do as she says," Curtis said, nudging Ralph. They both went into the dining room and joined Maureen. Ralph was surprised by the elaborate table furnishings.

17

"You sit here, Ralph," Maureen said pointing to a chair. After everyone was seated, Curtis said grace. When the food was passed around the table, Ralph thanked Maureen for what she had prepared.

"Maureen, the broiled salmon and broccoli is one of my favorite dishes," he commented.

The dinner was not only delicious, but was topped by one of Ralph's favorite desserts, strawberry pie. After dinner was over, Ralph complimented Maureen saying, "I enjoyed dinner very much. Thanks for having me."

"I'm glad you enjoyed the meal," she replied. Maureen then served each of them a cup of coffee and they remained at the table relaxing and talking over their good times together.

"Ralph, are you going to be all right?" she asked.

"Yes Maureen, I'll be okay. I have to admit it's been a shock," he replied.

"Ralph, we're friends. You look so sad. Can we be of help?" offered Maureen.

He responded by saying, "You know that when you lose someone who has been so good to you and your kids, it's hard to accept the reality of your loss. It's as if we were traveling down a road together and suddenly the road collapsed from under and she fell out and went down a cliff and I couldn't do anything to save her. She's gone."

Ralph continued, "Yes, Rosalie talked of dying during those last days we had together, and she is no longer suffering. She is at peace. When the kids left to return to live their lives with their families, I was alone. The shock turned to numbness. I went back to work and tried to stay active in the community. Everything seemed to be all right until I went home and faced a house that one time had been a home. No one was there, no one to share with. It was terrible. I soon felt the pangs of loneliness and I became melancholy."

"Have you ever considered getting help, a support group for those experiencing the same feelings you have?" Maureen asked, then added, "Sharing problems and concerns can provide some consolation."

"Come to think of it, Ralph, that's a great suggestion," Curtis said, then added, "You might want to give it a try." "I'll consider it, but I need some time," replied Ralph. "When you're ready, Reverend Harrigan may know of such a group that meets near by," Maureen offered. "Thanks. Thanks for dinner and your company. As much as I have enjoyed your hospitality, the hour is getting late. I'm still on the medication for the seizures that caused the accident. I do want to get home before dark," he explained.

"We were glad to have you for dinner. You know you're welcome anytime," Curtis said as he extended his arm to shake Ralph's hand. "You know, ole buddy, Maureen and I will stand by you. After all, that's what friends are for," he added.

And with these parting words, Ralph proceeded on the long trip home.

CHAPTER FIVE

The trip back home on Highway 73 brought back the discomforting memory of the accident he had experienced a year before. He recalled that he was in the process of installing siding on a new house, and had left his home in Newman's Center early on a Saturday morning. Highway 73 was slick with ice and he became more careful driving when he saw a number of cars in the median between the north and south lanes. As he approached the county reservoir, he suddenly became dizzy and passed out while driving. His car veered off to the left side of the highway, crossed the median and northbound lanes of Highway 73, struck a retaining wall of the reservoir, recrossed all four lanes of the highway, jumped a ditch, and then came to rest in a cornfield. He regained consciousness when a state trooper opened the driver's door and asked him how he was. When questioned regarding his name and occupation, he was disoriented.

At the hospital, the doctors in the emergency room checked his vital signs, and they were normal.

The hospital had called Rosalie and she came accompanied by Maureen. She was visibly upset, but relieved that he had not suffered any injuries. It was suggested that he see a doctor to determine the cause of the dizziness and the loss of consciousness.

Doctor Conrad, the family physician, felt the dosage of his blood pressure medication was responsible for what had happened. Even though Ralph was feeling well, he began to have similar experiences passing out, even in his office at the college at his desk. At Doctor Conrad's request, he began a series of tests that failed to determine the cause of what the medical profession called seizures.

First the blood sugar test, then heart medication, and finally the preparation for heart surgery. However, the results of the tests ruled out the operation. It appeared to him that the medical profession used the trial approach to find the real cause. A neurologist at the hospital suggested medication to prevent seizures. It appeared to be working since he had no recurrence of the seizures.

Ralph found himself turning into the driveway. He was home. The garage door opened and he parked the car inside. After getting out of his car, he walked to the inside service door, pressed a button to close the garage door, then unlocked the door to the house. He walked through the laundry room and kitchen and started to pass through into the living room. He stopped and glancing around, realized that he was home and lonely again.

CHAPTER SIX '

He stopped at the top step of the sunken living room and gazed out of the bay window overlooking a wooded ravine. He began to reminisce. Rosalie had wanted to select the house they were to live in when the trustees insisted that they move to Vernon Heights. After looking in the area, they could not find a house that was affordable nor one that would be comfortable, so they decided to build. In that way, much of the work could be done by them, not only cutting costs, but they would end up with a house to their liking.

Rosalie obtained house plan books from the bookstore at the shopping center and began looking for a desirable plan. When she found one, Ralph immediately sent for the plans. The next thing to do was to find a lot and sell the house they were living in. It was like starting over again as they had when they were first married.

Ralph and Rosalie began looking for the perfect lot, and finally, after an exhausting day in this effort, decided to purchase one of the last lots they had looked at. He remembered when they staked out the area where the house would be located on the lot, working together on various phases of construction, to build a house that they had never seen. Many of the workmen who were hired to perform the skilled tasks needed to build a house were very helpful to them, and Rosalie would show gratitude by making sure there was a full pot of coffee for them at all times. The staining of the woodwork and the painting of the entire interior of the house stood out more now than ever before. It was her work and she had been there to complete it, but now she was gone.

He kept thinking of the deep and abiding joy they shared together. As she lifted the cup of joy and drank from it, so also did she meet sorrow and pain. She accepted the fact that she was going to die. She endured the agony because there was no cure for an illness that enslaved her and dominated her until she succumbed to it.

His loneliness became more intense, and with it the pain and melancholy.

CHAPTER SEVEN

Ralph returned to work the next morning. His mind continued to wander in the past. It was not too long ago that the trustees had extended his contract and he and Rosalie were beginning to feel comfortable in the community. She was making friends with people who shared common interests. This made the transition from Newman's Center much easier.

With everything going so well for them, it was alarming when Rosalie discovered a lump in one of her breasts. She went immediately to Dr. Conrad to have it checked. She and Ralph were worried, and prayed that it would not be a cancerous tumor. Dr. Conrad felt surgery was necessary, as quickly as arrangements could be made.

After the operation, the biopsy determined that it was cancer, and further tests were taken. It was the consensus of the medical team that chemotherapy begin. It was not long until she became weak and the pain was so excruciating that she was admitted to the hospital's special oncology unit.

She feared being alone and she asked Ralph, ''Please get someone to ease the pain by rubbing my back and my legs.''

He assured her that he would. The next day he called the County Nurses' Association, which was able to provide nursing care at an additional cost. It didn't make any difference. Because they were experiencing a shortage of nurses, they were only able to provide two shifts of nurses. The eleven p.m. to seven a.m. shift could not be covered. The nurses felt that she would be sleeping during that time and the regular hospital nursing staff would be able to handle the situation. Rosalie pleaded with Ralph to stay during that time.

"You can sleep in one of the conference rooms that has a couch," she suggested. "If I need you, one of the nurses can get you."

But Ralph chose to sleep in the room, making a bed by placing two upholstered chairs front to front and using several pillows furnished by the hospital nurses to cushion his head.

It was during this time that he and Rosalie had reminisced on their life with one another. They talked of the happy times they both shared with the children, watching them as they grew up.

Rosalie asked, "Ralph, would you recite that poem you used to say when we were going together?"

She was referring to several of the verses from the poem *Annabelle Lee*, by Edgar Allan Poe, using her name in the place of Annabelle Lee. He obliged her by reciting those verses which he had intoned so romantically when he was courting her:

> *"There once was a maiden whom you may know*
> *By the name of Rosalie.*
> *She was a child, and I was a child*
> *In this kingdom by the sea,*
> *But we loved with a love that was more*
> *Than love, I and my Rosalie.*
> *With a love that the winged seraphs of heaven*
> *coveted, her and me."*

During that time there was hope for her eventual recovery. She was now able to sit up in bed and move her legs without pain.

25

The doctors told Ralph the cancer had spread to her spine, causing the pain in her legs and her lack of mobility. There was hope that the treatment she was receiving would prevent the cancer from attacking the nervous system. If that occurred, the cancer would go into remission.

Ralph remembered her delight one evening when he came to see her. She burst out enthusiastically, saying, "Ralph, I can sit up now — the pain isn't as bad." She added with some disappointment, "I still can't move my legs though."

He encouraged her by saying, "Rosalie, just keep it up — keep trying. Even if you have to be in a wheelchair — it makes no difference to me, as long as we are happy together. We can still live for each other."

She began to talk of death and her wishes after she passed on. "We've been good to each other, but Ralph, you must continue. Make a life for yourself. You will need someone, so find that right person and get married again. You should be happy."

"Oh," Ralph retorted. "Don't even talk like that. You're going to get well."

She had praise for the work of the young nurses from the County Nurses' Association and the help they provided. They would rub her legs, alleviating the pain. They treated her very well. Rosalie was happy. Everyone was doing everything they could. Ralph was beginning to become optimistic, looking forward to the day when Rosalie would be able to leave her bed and get into a wheelchair.

But it was not meant to be. That fateful morning when he received the call from the hospital requesting that he come immediately, he knew it was over.

"With a love that the winged seraphs
Of heaven coveted her and me.
And that is the reason a wind blew out of
A cloud one night, chilling and killing
My Rosalie."

He caught himself. He must be prepared to speak to a business and community group at lunch time. It was difficult for him to focus on the topics he wanted to address in the talk. His train of thought was clouded by the events of the recent past. Perhaps Maureen was right. A support group might help him. It may be worth a try. He would call when he returned to the office.

At lunch, he was introduced by Paul Hardy, an executive of a small machine and tool corporation. Ralph stressed the severe constraints of the economy and the problems of a future workforce as we approach the next century.

"We are in a technological revolution, comparable to the industrial revolution of the early 1900s. However, there does not appear to be the driving force that even recognizes what skills are needed for the workforce in the year 2000. He referred to an article from the Washington Post dated December 1, 1986, which quoted the Secretary of Labor, William E. Brock, as follows:

". . . . . the job creation capability of this country is so awesome that we have, in the next seven or eight years, a chance to deal with societal problems, such as youth unemployment, minority unemployment . . . . . The demand is going to be enormous. The demand for people with skills is going to be huge. And the question is, do we have in place the systems, the processes, to provide these skills?"

Then he quoted a passage from the State of the Union Address by President Ronald Reagan in 1987 in which he said, "The quest for excellence into the 21st century begins in the schoolroom, but must go next to the workplace. More than 20 million new jobs will be created before the new century unfolds, and by then our economy should be able to provide a job for everyone who wants to work. We must also enable our workers to adapt to the rapidly changing nature of the workplace."

Ralph continued, "The delivery system is in place if we can meet the challenges to provide math, science, and communication skills along with the occupational and critical thinking skills that will supply the workforce with more knowledgeable employees.

"Employees would then be able to adapt to more sophisticated changes in technology — thus increasing production, stabilizing the economy of the community, and thereby greatly improving the quality of life. We are not training humans to be robots just because of the notion that they can work with their hands. We are educating human beings so that their growth will have a positive impact on our society."

On the way back to his office, Ralph was thinking of his loneliness. Perhaps he should take the bull by the horns and check into a support group. He finally admitted to himself that he needed help.

The next morning, Ralph contacted Father Joseph Edwards, pastor of Saint Agnes Catholic Church in Clarion, a larger city south of Vernon Heights. He was inquiring about a support group for those who have suffered the loss of a mate.

Father Edwards was very encouraging when he said, "We'll look forward to seeing you at 7:30 on Tuesday evening, Mr. Steele."

CHAPTER EIGHT

Ralph drove to Clarion and into the parking lot of St. Agnes church and sat in his car. He was confused and unsure of what he was doing. He believed that he needed help, and he was determined to give the support group a chance. He got out of his car and walked to the entrance of the chuch hall. As he opened the door, he heard voices. Ralph quickly closed the door and returned to his car. Once inside, he began to put the key in the ignition but began to think — why?

He needed help, so he should take advantage of this opportunity. He was like the drowning man who would grasp at a straw to save his life. He decided he should go through with it.

He got out of his car again and walked into the church hall. He was greeted by the two facilitators of the group, Julia Woods and James Martin.

Julia tried to ease his discomfort, ''You're Mr. Steele,'' seeming to recognize him.

''Yes,'' he replied, showing surprise that she would know him without ever having met him.

She explained, "I attended a workshop at the college last fall, and I remember seeing you then. Father Edwards told me that you would be attending. I'm sorry to hear about your wife, but let's hope we can help you here," she added.

Julia Woods was divorced and in her late forties. Her husband had had numerous affairs while their children were growing up. When the children became old enough to be on their own, and the affairs and carousing continued, she obtained a divorce.

"I'll introduce you to James Martin, who helps me at these sessions," she said. "Jim, this is Ralph Steele, the dean of technical education at the college in Vernon Heights."

Jim Martin, who appeared to be in his early forties and was very well groomed, extended his hand to Ralph. Then he put his arm around Ralph's shoulders and said, "Look, we're here to help as much as possible. We all have suffered losses. Take me for instance. I married when I was a teenager and three years later lost my wife in a car accident. I have never remarried."

"Have a seat Ralph," he offered, then asked, "May I call you Ralph?"

"Yes," chimed in Julia. "Everyone calls each other by their first name. It's part of the therapy," she explained.

"When the rest of the group shows up we can start," said Jim, and added, "In the meantime, have a cup of coffee." He pointed to a table with a coffee urn, cups and condiments.

Ralph was not one to turn down a cup of coffee. He picked up a cup and opened the spout of the urn until the coffee reached the top. He knew he had drawn too much so he sipped some and returned to his chair.

A short time later, two other men showed up and sat down, waiting for the meeting to begin. Everyone appeared nervous, so Ralph assumed that it must have been the first meeting for all three men.

As he was looking around and assessing the situation, Father Edwards came in and greeted everyone with "Good evening."

He was a tall, slender man in his early fifties, very distinguished looking with his neatly combed gray hair. He waved his arm to get everyone's attention, then said, "Let's begin with a prayer."

When he finished, Father Edwards introduced Julia Woods and Jim Martin. Everyone then introduced themselves. Ralph later learned that Marlon Andrews, a man in his early fifties, had recently celebrated his 25th wedding anniversary. His wife was a volunteer at their church in the rural area of Powhattan, and had become infatuated with one of the deacons of the church. The two of them divorced their spouses and ran off and were married, somewhere out west. This really shook Marlon up, and he said that he was lonely.

Harvey Mitchell, who also was in his fifties, worked in a factory. His wife also worked there in another department. She began to chase around with one of Harvey's friends who worked with him at the factory. Everyone knew, even his three grown children. One day she packed up her belongings and left. They later divorced, but he had been extremely bitter because he had never been able to accept the reality of the divorce.

George Stevens, a widower, was a World War II veteran in his early sixties. It was difficult for him to walk on his right leg because of wounds from schrapnel. His wife died of heart disease a year previously, after forty years of marriage. He too experienced a feeling of loneliness.

Julia Woods began the session. She said, "You know, it's really hard to cope with the loss of a loved one. The loss of a person has many faces. It is something that each and every one of us must experience some time in our life. The loss may be a divorce — the breakup perhaps of a long marriage. It can cause bitterness and resentment, especially if you have kept your wedding vows and made every effort to make the marriage work.

"The loss of a spouse through death often times is a loss that turns the world topsy turvy for the person left behind. Grief over the loss of the loved one can cause a deep seated state of loneliness that is difficult to overcome. One way is

31

to begin to live your life over again. With these losses, the symptoms are stress, anger, feelings of helplessness, depression, frustration, anxiety, and above all — loneliness.''

She continued, ''A loss through divorce or death will cause immediate shock and numbness. This is usually followed by frustration, loneliness, anger, guilt, and denial. Sometimes there will be the inability to be logical. Symptoms of physical illness, depression, bizarre behavior, and difficulty with having normal relationships often occur. But a person can recover if he accepts the reality of what has happened, and be positive in everything he does. In short, think positive, act positive, and be positive. And now Jim will continue.''

Jim began, ''You know fellows, I lost a wife in an automobile accident. Even though we had been married a short time and had no children, I remember the loneliness, because ours had been a special kind of love and companionship that exists between two people who care about one another and are willing to share one another.

''One of the things you're going to have to do is get serious about starting your life over again. That means beginning to meet people of the opposite sex. Socializing will help a great deal because you will begin to interact with someone else, even if it's only friendly conversation, sitting down and having a drink, be it coffee or a beer, or going to a dance. It can help.

''I would like to suggest that all of us, including Julia, attend the singles dance this Sunday at the Clarion Hotel. It starts at eight p.m. They hold it every Sunday evening strictly for single people like us. Let's all plan on being there this Sunday. We can all sit at the same table and support one another. This can be the first step away from loneliness.''

Everyone nodded in agreement that they would be there. Ralph would also be there.

CHAPTER NINE

Ralph pulled into the parking lot of the Clarion Hotel. He looked at his watch and saw that he was early. He wondered if he should go in. He was uneasy about attending this dance in the first place, but decided that anything was worth trying if it would stop that ugly feeling of loneliness. He proceeded inside and saw a group of women in the hotel lobby sitting and talking to each other. As he stepped inside the door, they stopped talking and looked at him. Two younger women, who were sitting together on a couch at the far end of the lobby, began to giggle. He became nervous about what he had confronted, abruptly turned around and returned to the outside. He felt very uncomfortable and decided it would be best if he went home. He walked to his car and began to unlock the car door when Jim Martin pulled into the parking lot and yelled out of his car window, "Hey Ralph, you're early. Wait for me and we can go in together."

Ralph felt relieved as he watched Jim get out of his car and begin walking toward him. Then with an arm around

Ralph's shoulder, he said, "Come on, let's go in and wait for the others inside."

They went into the hotel lobby and sat down. Ralph thought it amusing that he was now sitting in the same room with the women who earlier had made him feel so self-conscious. Ten minutes later, Julia Woods came in with Harvey Mitchell and Marlon Andrews. Julia had found them wandering in the parking lot debating between themselves whether to come in.

They were not alone, Ralph thought. This was a new experience and not easy to get accustomed to.

"Where's George Stevens?" Jim asked. "Did you see him in the parking lot?"

"No," replied Julia.

Jim continued, "It's just about time for the dance to begin. Why don't you take the guys and get a table so we can all sit together. I'll go out in the parking lot and see if George may be late or just sitting in his car waiting for us."

"Okay, Jim. Sounds like a good idea," replied Julia. She motioned for them to follow her down a hallway to the ballroom where the dance was being held. As they walked down the hallway, Ralph noticed the halls were decorated with tapestry depicting each of the Roman gods.

Soon they came upon two men and two women seated at a table. Each appeared to have a certain responsibility. First each one was to fill out an information card. This would be kept on file so on any return visit the cost of admission would only be $5. First-time visits cost $10. There was also a drawing for free dance lessons that each participant could enter by filling out a slip and placing it through a slot in a cardboard box. There was one woman who was in charge of the money box and handled the admission charge. Everyone commented about the paper work required just to get into a dance. What next, they all thought.

Jim returned without George who was nowhere to be found in the parking lot. They proceeded into the ballroom. Julia spotted a round table with eight chairs. "What do you think?" she asked as she gestured to the table she had selected. "Let's sit here."

"Fine with me," they all said in unison.

The room was beginning to fill with men and women all dressed in what appeared to be their finest clothes. It was like a charade since you could detect the sad look of loneliness and despair.

The disc jockey began to put tapes into his machine and the music started. Immediately the dance floor began to fill with couples. As they moved across the floor to the beat of the music, there was laughter and people began to smile. They seemed to be enjoying themselves.

There were cash bars at each end of the room. Ralph asked if anyone wanted anything from the bar. Marlon offered to help him by saying, "Ralph, let's get everybody's order, and then we'll go and get the drinks." Everyone quickly decided on diet cola, which made it easy to remember. After they returned with the drinks and placed them on the table, Ralph sat down and began sipping his drink as he watched the couples dance, apparently having fun even though they may have had similar reasons for being as lonely as he was.

Then came the cry, "Ladies Choice."

As she stood up, Julia said to Ralph, "You're not sure about all of this, so why not dance?"

Julia had come to his rescue again, Ralph thought. He remembered when he came to the first meeting of the support group and it was Julia who sensed his uneasiness and was able to help him mingle with the group.

"All right, Julia," replied Ralph, "let me warn you that I'm a country boy with two left feet when I dance."

"Oh, come on!" she said as she grabbed his hand and pulled him up from his chair to the floor.

With Ralph following behind Julia, he noticed that she was an attractive woman. She was tall and slim, and the sensual beauty of her body made him want to take her into his arms.

As she turned to dance, he noticed for the first time the daring cut of her dress which exposed her shoulders and the top of her large round breasts. Her face was heart-shaped with a dainty straight nose, her mouth generously ripe, and her eyes were wide, large and deep blue.

"Well, let's begin," she said.

"I warned you that I had two left feet and can't dance too well," he said sheepishly.

"Let's do it any way," Julia coaxed.

As he took her into his arms to dance, he could smell the perfume on her skin and in the light brown hair that fell to her shoulders. He could feel her breasts on his chest. At the end of the dance, she stepped back and said, "That was great, Ralph. Promise me you'll dance with me again?" she asked.

"Thank you very much," he replied, as they held both hands out in front of them. "I'll take you up on having another dance with me," he said.

He followed her back to the table and watched the sensual movement of her slim body. She was gorgeous. During the course of the evening, Julia danced with Harvey and Marlon. Each time she left the table to go to the dance floor, Ralph could not help but enjoy the curves of her slender body as she walked. As she was dancing, he could see her moving in rhythm to the music. Her soft feminine charm attracted Ralph as he watched her every dance.

And then the cry, "Men's Choice."

Before he could get the words out of his mouth, Marlon Andrews asked her to dance. As they went to the floor and danced, Ralph sat sipping on his cola watching Julia. That had been the last dance, and everyone was getting up and leaving.

Ralph got up from the table, and as he left the room he bid the group, "So long, see you next Tuesday."

He walked out of the hotel and to his car in the parking lot. As he got into his car, his heart was throbbing, as a young teenager would feel when excited by the sensual beauty and feminine allure of an attractive woman.

CHAPTER TEN

It was a Tuesday morning. Ralph got up to get an early start for the day ahead. While he was shaving, he thought of his upcoming meeting with the industrial council. He had prepared information to present to them which had mainly been precipitated by the talk he had given earlier. Hc and his secretary, Violet, put together illustrations on flip charts for the Workforce 2000 presentation that he was going to use.

The material that he would cover, he thought, would be the survey of labor shortages, the education required for the jobs in the year 2000, and a list of the fastest growing jobs, all statistics of the U.S. Bureau of Labor. He was looking forward to this presentation since it fell right in line with the proposal that he was working on to upgrade the curriculum and admissions standards requiring higher academic skills, with the hope of bringing more students to the college who could successfully meet the needs of the workforce in the community.

Curtis Sims was one of several members of the staff at the college who thought that business and industry had sufficient resources to train their employees.

Ralph had been in the private sector as a small business-man, and there was sharp disagreement since this group of academicians did not realize that small and individual businesses do not have the time and resources to train employees, when that responsibility lays in the hands of formal education, both public and private.

Suddenly, while shaving, he felt drowsy and decided to sit on a stool in the bedroom until he felt better. He blacked out. When he regained consciousness, he laid on the floor with his nose bleeding profusely. He had had another seizure, he was thinking, but could not understand why, since he was taking the medication which had been prescribed to him after the accident. He stopped the nose bleed by dousing cold water on his face and holding cold washcloths to his nose. He later discovered that he had fallen against the bedpost and hit his nose against it.

He felt weak and decided to call Violet Swanson. "Violet, this is Mr. Steele," he said. "An urgent matter has come up which I must attend to. Would you please get the flip charts ready for me to pick up around eleven on my way to the industrial council meeting?"

"Yes, Mr. Steele, everything will be ready for you when you come in," she said.

He thanked her and immediately called Dr. Conrad to report what had happened. He was not available, so he told the nurse who had answered the phone about his seizure.

"I'll have the doctor get back to you as soon as he gets done with the patient he's with now," she said.

Ralph was growing impatient waiting for Dr. Conrad to return his call. Finally the phone rang and it was Dr. Conrad. "Ralph," he said, "I hear that you've had another seizure."

"Yes," replied Ralph, and added, "I hope we can get to the bottom of this. I've been taking the medication."

"I'm going to contact a neurologist to whom I've referred patients in the past. I'm going to ask him if he'll do some testing on you to determine what has developed. His name is Dr. Arthur Pare. Jenny, my nurse, will call right away and make an appointment. She'll get back to you to give you details."

38

"Thank you very much, Dr. Conrad. I'll be waiting for the call," he replied.

Looking at the clock on the wall, it was ten minutes before ten o'clock. He still had some time to wait for a call from Dr. Conrad's office before he would have to leave for the office.

His thoughts focused on the way Curtis Sims was acting. Until recently, he was able to depend on him for support. As long as they had known one another, their views on job training were the same. That was one of the reasons he had supported Curtis for a position at the college when an opening became available. He remembered some time ago one of the staff members warning him that Curtis was after his job. At the time he dismissed the comment, and with the support that both he and Maureen had given him after Rosalie's death, it was difficult for him to comprehend.

The phone rang and he picked it up on the second ring. "Hello," he said.

It was Jenny from Dr. Conrad's office. "Mr. Steele, we've arranged an MRI Cat-Scan for you on Thursday morning at eight o'clock in the Radiology Lab at St. Mary's Hospital in Clarion. Is that time all right with you?" she asked.

"Yes, I'll write it down in my appointment book," he replied as he reached for his appointment book lying on the desk beside the phone.

"Thank you for your help. I feel more comfortable knowing that I may find out what's causing these seizures. Thanks again," he said.

"Well, you have a good day. Mr. Steele," she replied.

It was time for Ralph to leave, and he moved gingerly as he got into his car. He was feeling much better. He stopped by the office to pick up the materials for his presentation. He thanked Violet for her help and efficiency as he left the office.

At the restaurant, he talked with a number of CEO's and human relations directors. They all were citing examples of their inability to obtain good entry-level employees who could be productive for their companies.

John Abner, who was owner of a local machine and tool shop, asked, "Did you know the average age of tool-&-die makers in this country is 59 years old? That means we are losing some of these men to retirement every year. The problem is there are no bright machinists coming up who can benefit from the knowledge and "tricks of the trade" these men possess," he said.

"We're in for a tough row to hoe if we don't get out young people interested in this vital occupation," he added. After lunch Ralph began his presentation. He had already set up his flip charts which showed the survey of employers regarding the labor shortage we were experiencing that would effect us into the next century. Technicians were most in demand. The chart also illustrated the need for those in professional occupations, supervisory and management, secretary/clerical, skilled trades, sales, and administrative positions.

His second chart emphasized the tragedy of the American family. In 1955, 60 percent of American households consisted of the traditional working father, mother at home, and two or more children in the family. By 1980 only 11 percent of all households fit this pattern, and by 1986, the figure had fallen to 4 percent. Families were more diverse and less stable than ever before.

His third chart dealt with the level of education that an employee would need for the average new job of the 1990s, which showed 14 years of formal education.

He told the group, "The fact that America is moving from the manufacturing age to the service industry indicates that very few of the new jobs that are created will be suited for those who cannot read, follow directions, use mathematics, or do not possess good communication and critical thinking skills. We must address this issue by counseling our youth to pursue education that will lead them to the job opportunities that are out there for them."

Those on the council were pleased that Ralph was working on a plan to enhance the educational program at the college, and offered their support.

"I'm excited about the goals you are working toward," Rose Matthews said. "If I can be of any help to promote this concept, please call me at the office, Ralph."

"Thank you," he replied.

Rose worked at a real estate office, and was considered to be one of their outstanding sales persons.

There appeared to be a great deal of support, especially from John Abner, who said, "Ralph, I'm sure I speak for those who are here that when it's completed we'd like to see the proposal that you are preparing for the trustees." Everyone left looking forward to the next meeting of the industrial council.

Thursday morning Ralph went to St. Mary's Hospital in Clarion for his MRI test. It was an unusual test, as the patient was placed on a platform which was attached to a track. The platform on which the patient was strapped was then rolled into a cylinder barely large enough for the shoulders of the patient to fit into. In the case with Ralph, his head was placed into a harness, so there would be no movement during the test, which took approximately 45 minutes.

The following day he called Doctor Pare's office and asked for the results of his MRI.

"Sorry, Mr. Steele, but the doctor will have to call you and give you the results," was the reply.

All during the day Ralph agonized as to what the problem might be. He went home, but could not eat for he was too nervous.

At 7 o'clock in the evening the phone rang. Ralph rushed to answer it. "Hello," he said.

Dr. Pare was on the other end. "Mr. Steele, I have the results of the MRI scan you took Thursday. The scan shows an almond-sized tumor in the right temple area."

"Is it cancer?" Ralph asked.

"We can't tell. It's going to have to come out as soon as we can get you scheduled into the hospital. I need to call Allan Brown, who is an excellent neurosurgeon, to see what his schedule is like. As soon as I make the necessary arrangements, I'll give you a call. Will you be home this weekend?" he asked.

"Yes," replied Ralph, then added, "This is important to me. I'll definitely be here."

"Okay. You can expect a call from me sometime this weekend," Dr. Pare assured him.

Ralph was taken aback by the bad news: brain surgery and possible cancer. He had seen what it had done to Rosalie, and he was scared.

Saturday afternoon, Dr. Pare called and sounded very pleasant. "Mr. Steele, you can report to St. Mary's Hospital Monday at 8 o'clock in the morning. We've got you scheduled for tests on Monday and Tuesday. Wednesday at 7 o'clock in the morning you'll go to surgery," he said.

"I'll report to the patient desk Monday morning at 8:00. Thank you for calling and letting me know. I feel much better now," Ralph replied.

He immediately called Miles Weller, chairman of the trustees. "Mr. Weller, this is Ralph Steele. I called to let you know that I'm due to have surgery next Wednesday. An MRI that I took Thursday shows that I have an almond-sized tumor in my right temple. The doctors want me in the hospital Monday morning because they want to perform some tests on me. I'll call Curtis Sims so that he can cover for me."

"Well Ralph, I hope that it's nothing serious, and you'll be all right. Our prayers will be with you." Tears came to Ralph's eyes as he slowly lowered the receiver to its cradle. When he regained his composure, he called Curtis Sims and his secretary, Violet Swanson. He assured them that he would have a telephone in his room and they could contact him if there were any problems.

The most difficult thing he had to do was call his children. He assured them that things would be all right, that he was positive about the operation.

And now to prepare for Monday.

CHAPTER ELEVEN

Curtis Sims was assuming some of the duties of his old neighbor and friend, Ralph Steele. He was aware that Ralph had entered the hospital and was about to undergo surgery. One of the first things he did was to check with Ralph's secretary.

"Violet," he said. "Mr. Steele has asked me to attend any meetings he had scheduled, and to respond to any concerns that might arise."

"Oh, so Mr. Steele has gone to the hospital. Do you know which one?" she asked.

"St. Mary's, in Clarion," he replied.

"Then I'll send flowers on behalf of the college," she said.

"Mr. Sims, there is a meeting scheduled Wednesday with the industrial council. It'll be held at Jeffers' Steak House and starts at 11:30. If there are any notes that Mr. Steele left on his desk that he wanted to discuss, I'll get them to your office."

"I'll just jot that down in my appointment book," said Curtis, as he reached into his vest pocket and pulled out a blue book. Then he added, "Violet, you are very efficient. Let's work together while Mr. Steele is gone so that we can keep the college running smoothly."

When Curtis returned to his office, there was a call waiting for him from the chairman of the trustees of the College.

"Curtis, this is Miles Weller. I just want to verify that you and Ralph had a conversation regarding his absence while he's in the hospital," he chairman asked.

"Yes, Mr. Weller. I'm going to cover for him so we can continue to operate without any hitches," was the reply.

"Just one thing, Curtis. If any problems arise that need my help or I need to be informed of, call me," he offered.

It was Wednesday, and Curtis was planning to attend the meeting of the industrial council. According to what Ralph had told him, he was to have surgery early that morning. He was sure there would be some word on Ralph's condition later in the day. He then drove to Jeffers' Steak House and went in. He asked one of the waitresses, "Where is the industrial council meeting going to be held?"

"Right in that room," she replied, pointing to one of the party rooms.

Inside the room, there were two long tables set with plates, cups, and silverware. A waitress was filling glasses at each place setting with water and ice. Curtis walked up to several people standing in the center of the room.

"Hello, I'm Curtis Sims, from the college. I'm taking Ralph Steele's place while he's in the hospital having surgery," he said as he gestured to shake hands. This aroused the curiosity of the group.

"Is it serious?" asked Paul Hardy, who was one of the prime movers of the council and one of Ralph's supporters.

"He went into surgery this morning for a hemorrhage in his brain. He's in St. Mary's Hospital in Clarion," Curtis offered.

"Is there anything we can do?" they asked.

"I don't know of anything, but I'll keep in touch with you," Curtis assured them.

Everyone was startled by the news. They quickly ate and postponed any discussion until there was word of Ralph's condition.

"You will let us know, Mr. Sims, as soon as you hear?" Paul Hardy asked Curtis, as they left the restaurant.

CHAPTER TWELVE

It was Thursday morning and Ralph awoke to the bustling of the custodians moving their cleaning equipment down the hall. The sun shined through the window, brightening the room. He realized that he was in a hospital room. His head hurt and when he raised his hand to his brow, he discovered the bandage that surrounded his head from the ears up. A nurse came into the room carrying a tray with two small cups on it.

"Good morning, Mr. Steele," she greeted in a pleasant voice. "How do you feel?"

"I have a headache," he answered in a groggy tone.

"Well, I have something here that will make you feel better," she said as she lowered the tray and removed one of the cups and placed it to his lips. "Now open up and drink this," she said as she tipped the cup to his mouth. He swallowed the thick milky substance which tasted like peppermint.

"Very good. Now I have two pain pills that you have to take," she said as she placed the other cup with the pills to his open mouth. "I'll give you some water to help you

46

swallow.'' She reached for the water glass sitting on a table alongside the bed and he moved his arms in a position so his hands could catch the glass as it was moving to his mouth. When he was able to hold the glass and drink water from it, she let go and said, "Very good, Mr. Steele. You're going to get along just fine. I'm Ann Clark and I will be your nurse for this shift.'' she added.

"What time is it?'' he asked.

"You've been under for quite a long time. It's Thursday morning," she replied.

"Did everything turn out all right?'' he asked.

"You're doing well. I saw Dr. Brown and Dr. Pare out by the desk a little while ago. I'm sure they'll be in to see you soon,'' she replied.

As she moved around the room, he could not help but notice her body of medium build, very trim and athletic looking. The top buttons of her uniform were unbuttoned. What was he doing, measuring every woman's body? This young lady was young enough to be his daughter, yet he was imagining sexual pleasure with her. The devil made him do it, he joked to himself. As the nurse was leaving, Dr. Pare entered the room.

"Good morning, Ralph,'' he greeted. "You've had a rough time of it, but you came through the operation with flying colors. We watched you very closely because of your age, but you responded well, so Dr. Brown was able to perform the surgery with ease. The hospital pathologist had identified the tumor as infected tissue, possibly caused by a virus, but to be sure, we sent the tissue to another lab for a second opinion,'' he explained.

"Then it's not cancer,'' Ralph sighed in relief.

"Let's wait and be sure, but it did not show cancer in the tests here at the hospital,'' he cautioned. Ralph was feeling good. This was good news and inside he was thanking God.

"What now, doctor?'' Ralph asked.

"Well, we'll keep you in the hospital for a week and then let you go home, but we expect you to convalesce for at least

47

a month at home. In the meantime, I'll want you to continue your medication, including pain pills to help you with any discomfort you may have," he replied, then added, "In the meantime, relax. Remember it wasn't a tooth that was pulled. You had major surgery, and it will be some time before you'll be at full strength."

"Thank you doctor, I understand," Ralph said.

A lot had happened since he checked into the hospital admitting room on Monday. There were many tests that had been performed before he went into surgery. Another MRI, an EKG, EEG, numerous X-rays of his body, and blood tests were among the many that he somehow suffered through. And now it was over. He would lay back in comfort and enjoy the hospitality of a hospital, he mused.

He dozed off, but was awakened by the ring of the telephone. It surprised him, but he followed the ring to a table alongside his bed. He reached for the receiver and picked it up.

"Hello," he said.

"Is this Ralph Steele?" asked the person on the other end. He answered. "Yes." It was the voice of a female. He wondered if anything had gone wrong at the office. He didn't recognize the voice of Violet Swanson, his secretary.

"This is Julia Woods."

He was surprised and mumbled an "Ohhh."

"I heard that you were in the hospital. Are you okay?" she asked.

"I had surgery yesterday. I'm still a little groggy, but I'm beginning to feel much better," he replied, adding, "It's so very thoughtful of you to call."

"Can you have visitors?" she asked.

"I don't know for sure, but I feel well enough to dance," he chuckled.

"Good. Then you'll want someone to visit with you," she responded in an amusing tone. "I'll check with the desk, and if they say it's okay, you may have some visitors this evening. Jim and some of the men in the support group expressed concern for you, and perhaps they'll join me for a visit this evening during visiting hours."

"That'll be great," he said excitedly. "I'm looking forward to seeing you."

"See you later," she said as she ended the conversation.

Ralph was feeling ecstatic. The doctor had given him some good news about the operation, and now Julia was coming for a visit, which brought a smile to his face.

He could hear the lunch carts making their way down the hallway. In a matter of minutes, an aide brought a tray into the room and set it on the table, which she adjusted to make it easier for him to reach.

"Here's your lunch, Mr. Steele," she said, uncovering the dishes. "If you need any help, just let us know by pushing the button there by your side," she offered.

"No, I think I can handle this," he said as he looked the tray of food over to see what was on it.

He was hungry and it did not take long to devour the baked white fish, scalloped potatoes, fresh green peas, and jello fruit salad. He pushed the portable table forward and slowly began to drink a glass of orange juice. When he finished, he curled up under the covers and went to sleep.

He woke up before supper and decided to call Eileen, his daughter, to tell her that everything was all right. He picked up the phone and dialed her number. The hospital operator came on the line and verified the call. He could hear the phone ring and after several rings, Eileen answered. He was excited when he told her the good news. "I feel great, especially when they didn't find cancer. Besides being very thorough, they will get a second opinion," he explained.

"We were wondering and praying that you would be okay. It's so good to hear from you, Dad," she replied.

"Would you do me a favor, Eileen, and call Elicia, Mark and Matthew and fill them in on my condition?" Ralph asked.

"Sure, Dad, I'll be glad to," she replied.

They both said goodbye with loving words and he promised that he would keep her informed.

After supper, he got up and went to the bathroom and washed up. He looked at himself in the mirror, and sure enough, he was wrapped like a mummy from the ears up. What a sight, he thought. At least he didn't have to comb his hair. On the way back to his bed, he located his suitcase and opened it. He reached into the pocket where he had packed his electric razor. He decided to return to the bathroom and use the mirror while he shaved. On the way back to the bed, he returned the shaver to the suitcase. He felt much better, and was ready for company.

Just as he pulled the covers to his chest, Miles Weller and his wife, Agnes, came in. "Hello Ralph," they greeted.

"Hello, nice to see you," replied Ralph.

"How are you feeling?" they asked.

"Like a million bucks. I know I may not look like much," Ralph explained, "But preliminary reports indicate that the tumor was not cancer, but infected tissue."

"That's great to hear," Miles said in a relieved tone.

Agnes asked, "How long will you have to stay in the hospital?"

"The doctor told me this morning I'd be in the hospital for a week, then I could go home to convalesce for at least a month," he answered.

"You'll be missed at the college," Miles said.

"When I get home, I believe I'll have the time to work on the proposal for the college to meet the needs of our community," Ralph said optimistically. He added, "I'll be in contact with my office in case I'm needed to make any decisions."

"Sounds to me like you plan to be on top of things. That's great," replied Miles.

They talked for some time and finally, Agnes said, "Don't you think we better go and let Ralph get his rest?"

"All right," replied Miles. Miles stood up and went to the edge of the bed and shook Ralph's hand. "We'll be going now, and take care of yourself. Do what the doctor says."

"Will do, and thanks for coming up to see me. It was very thoughtful of you," replied Ralph.

They both started to leave, and at the doorway they said in unison, "Bye now, and take care."

Ralph was glad that they came. He sank back into his bed and closed his eyes since he tired easily, and fell back asleep. A short time later he felt a kiss on his check, and someone squeezing his hand. He opened his eyes and saw that Julia Woods was standing by his bed. "I knew that little peck on the cheek would wake you," she mused.

"Oh, Julia, you look as pretty as ever," he replied.

"Thank you, Ralph," she said, "And how are you feeling?" she asked.

"Like a million dollars," he replied. A bit puzzled, he looked around and asked, "Where are the rest of the guys?"

"Ralph, when I contacted them, they all had commitments for tonight and didn't feel they could work it into their schedules," she explained. "But I decided to come anyway. They all asked me to wish you well."

"Julia, you're something else," he said as he extended his arms toward her. "Come, sit on the bed," he coaxed.

She took her coat off and sat on the edge of the bed. He placed his hands on her shoulders and said, "You are beautiful. It is so thoughtful of you to come and visit me."

"I wish I could be close to you and dance. You know you owe me a dance," he said.

"I know, Ralph. When you get out, we'll go dancing. It doesn't have to be at the Clarion Hotel. They have dancing at the Calumet Club on Wednesday and Thursday nights," she suggested.

She had that sensual air about her that aroused him. In a surprisingly short time, she had become an important person to him. "Julia," he said warmly, "You are very special to me. I'm attracted to you," drawing her to him and kissing her as she fell into his arms as he lay on the bed.

"And I am to you," she sighed.

They kissed again passionately as they looked into each other's eyes. "Ralph, dear. I have to go now, but I'll be back tomorrow," she said, digging into his shoulders with her fingers and kissing him again. She sat up on the bed and looked at him, placing her hand on one of his lips. "Until tomorrow, dear," she promised.

She got up from the bed, and as she was putting her outstretched arms into her coat, he relished her slim, curvaceous body. About to leave, she reached down and kissed him saying, "Bye love, till tomorrow."

He watched her as she drifted from the room, dreaming of her in his arms as they danced to slow music. His dreams were interrupted as he heard the night nurse walk briskly into the room with her tray. This time there were three cups of medication for him to take. He complied with the nurse and when she left, he snuggled under the covers and went to sleep.

CHAPTER THIRTEEN

Time passed quickly for Ralph's stay in the hospital. Julia visited every night as she had promised. They would walk to the cafeteria and sit and have a cup of coffee together, talking about the good times ahead. He told her about the project he was working on for the college.

"It's a proposal that's being prepared for presentation to the trustees," he explained, "but I only have a month to put it together."

"I'm proud of you, Ralph. Your attitude is so positive about finding a new life for yourself," she said.

"Now you must promise me that after my month of convalescing at home, that we'll go dancing," he asked.

"Maybe I will come and visit you before then," she paused, "that is, if I'm allowed to," she said with a look of eagerness.

"You sure are. I'd be glad to have you," he replied. They would return to his room and sit together on the bed, kissing passionately until it was time for her to go. When she left, he knew he would miss her, and anxiously awaited for her next visit.

The day came for him to be discharged. He received a prescription for the pain pills he had been taking at the hospital, along with instructions to follow during his stay at home. Dr. Brown, his neurosurgeon, wanted to see him in two weeks to remove the stitches from the incision. A week later Dr. Pare, his neurologist, wanted to see him. He was now free to go.

Ralph was home at last. He called Violet Swanson at the college to let her know he was home and if anything came up, she could call him there. "It's so nice to hear your voice," Violet said. "Some of us were concerned at first when Mr. Sims came in and told us you weren't looking too well," she added.

"Funny. I don't remember Curtis being there, Violet," replied Ralph, warily.

"I guess he was there right after you came out of intensive care and were just taken to your room," she explained.

"Well, I guess I was still under the influence of the anesthesia and wasn't supposed to be taking visitors yet," he said with a chuckle.

"Oh, Mr. Steele, it's good to hear you laugh. You still have your sense of humor!" she said.

"I'm going to start work putting together a proposal for the trustees. When I complete it, I'll need to have it typed," he said.

"You just call and let me know when you want it typed, and I'll get someone to pick it up," she replied.

"I'll do that Violet. Thanks."

He hung up, wondering about Curtis. Why hadn't he left a message or come back later? Oh well, that's the past. I'm going to concentrate on the future, he thought.

Ralph began work on his proposal in earnest, determined to catch up on lost time. He began it this way:

54

"By the year 2000, 80 percent of the jobs in America will require some type of specialized, technical skills. In addition, the vast majority of Americans will need to continually upgrade their skills in order to keep abreast of the ever-changing technology.

1. Transfer of credit agreements were presently in the process of being signed with one institution of higher learning and two more were in the negotiation stage. As these articulation agreements were signed, it would allow students to receive credit for course work taken at the business and technical college toward a baccalaureate degree at one of the universities in the area.

2. A Business, Industry, and Education Task Force would be establised to review and make recommendations in the following areas:

— retrain employee skills

— provide counseling and career choices to laid-off employees

— attract adults who have the potential of becoming productive employees and citizens for the technological future

— develop performance objectives for each course

— give each student an Individual Instructional Plan listing objectives and target dates for completion

— conduct periodic assessments

— develop close liaisons with the state Department of Development

3. The Task Force would make their recommendations to the college trustees.

When he was finished, he called Violet and made arrangements for the proposal to be picked up so that she could begin typing it. He called his friend, Rose Matthews, the real estate agent, and told her he was interested in selling his house.

"Ralph, will you be there this afternoon, say around four o'clock?" she asked.

"Yes, Rose," he replied.

It was noon, so he fixed a sandwich and opened a can of soup for lunch. There was plenty of diet cola in the refrigerator, so he opened a can and poured its contents into a glass. He dutifully swallowed his medication.

At 4 p.m. on the dot, the doorbell rang. It was Rose Matthews. "Hello, Ralph," she greeted. "Hope you're feeling better."

"I am. Come on in," he said as he motioned her through the doorway. "I know I look like a mummy, but in a week the bandages will come off. The only problem is I won't have much hair," he said playfully.

"Well, you still look good considering what you've been through," she replied.

"Thanks, Rose, I needed that."

"May I look around?" she inquired.

"Sure, go ahead," he answered.

She opened her notebook and said, "Perhaps we should complete the listing information first." She asked the usual questions regarding the number of bedrooms, whether or not there was a basement, the size of the lot, the water supply, etc. She observed the carpeting, oak floor entrance, and the deck running the length of the rear of the house.

"I'll look around now," she said.

He could not help but notice that she was dressed in a navy blue and white suit, the skirt just above the knees, accentuating her lean, well-toned legs as she walked around gracefully in a pair of dark blue heels. He caught himself looking at her with lust, admiring her legs. He sat down at the kitchen table, staring out the window.

In a short time she returned and stood at his side, a notebook in front of her as she turned toward him and said, "Ralph, let's go over the figures I've come up with." She sat at the table and moved her chair closer to him so they were side by side. "I suggest we list the house at $200,000 and go no lower than $180,000. I've checked recent sales in the area, and the average home this size has sold for $175,000, so we'd be in the price range."

Ralph replied, "Rose, you're the expert. I trust your judgment, so let's go for it."

She completed the listing agreement and Ralph signed it. "I have one other request, Rose," he said.

"And what is that?" she asked.

"I'd like you to locate an apartment for me as soon as possible. That way I'll be out of here and you can get in whenever you need to because you'll have a key."

"The idea sounds good, but a house shows better when it has furniture," she responded, adding, "We can put a lock box on a door, preferably the back door, so our sales personnel can gain entry."

"Well, let's go that way. But still keep in mind that I'll be needing an apartment," he said.

She left a copy of the listing agreement with Ralph, picked up her notebook, and walked to the door. Ralph opened the door for her as she said, "Well, thank you Ralph. Now you take care of yourself. You can be assured we'll be getting on this. So long."

Ralph waved goodbye, closed the door, and returned to the kitchen. He was not hungry, but it was getting near dinner time. He managed another sandwich, bowl of soup and a glass of milk. Later, he sat down in the family room and read the evening paper. Not much news he thought, so he turned the television on to listen to the national news and soon dozed off. He was awakened by the ring of the doorbell. He glanced at his watch as he rose from the chair and walked to the door. It was 8:30 in the evening.

He opened the door to a smiling Julia. "Hi!" she greeted.

"Hi, come in. Let me take your coat," he said as he reached for the coat as she slipped out of it. He hung it in the hall closet and turned to her saying, "What a pleasant surprise."

"I told you I'd come and visit! Now what will we do, watch television?" she asked with a gentle smile on her face. He suggested, "We don't have to watch TV. I could turn on the radio to one of those music stations and we could dance. The oak floored foyer and hallway would be a good surface to dance on. The radio is right here." He pointed to the radio and said, "You can select the station that has the music you

57

like. Remember, two left feet will attempt to dance to any kind of music."

She turned to a station with soft, slow music, and turned to him saying, "No one has asked me to dance."

He gravely intoned, "May I have this dance?"

Together they danced sensuously to several of the slow dances that were played. "Let's sit down," she murmured.

"Okay," he said as he swept her into the family room. As she paused in the doorway, he enfolded his arms around her, kissing her warmly. She responded passionately. Her passion grew stronger and he gently unbuttoned her blouse. She in turn unbuttoned his shirt, and then pressed her breasts against his chest. His lips came down upon hers fiercely and demandingly.

And then she cried out, "Ralph, I'm not ready for another relationship. We've gone too far. Let's be friends and keep it at that, okay?" She withdrew and began to button her blouse. She started to cry, saying, "I'm sorry, please forgive me for acting like this."

"But Julia, I started it," he apologized.

"But I aroused you. It wasn't fair of me to get carried away like I did," she said through her tears.

"Let's forget it ever happened. Why don't we sit at the kitchen table and I'll get us some diet cola," he replied. He went to a kitchen cabinet and took two glasses from the shelf, then went to the refrigerator and filled each one with ice, then poured diet cola into the glasses. He returned to the table and gave Julia her drink, setting his down in front of the chair where he would sit. Once positioned in his chair, he began to explain his behavior.

"Julia, I'm so very lonely that I'm not acting in a rational manner. Please don't think I'm giving excuses, but I have been used to a relationship for a long, long time. I know you counsel the support group and have experience in dealing with people like me, but let me tell you how I feel. It's as if I were traveling down this road with a partner of 36 years. The road is rocky at times, smooth most of the time, and there are times when the road is dangerous. But we still continue down this road until one day my partner slips off the side and down into a canyon. It is as though a part of me is gone — my life is empty, and has no meaning. There are no quick fixes or I'd try to fix it. It's like I've tried to explain to others: I feel like that drowning man who will grasp at straws just to save his life.''

"Ralph," replied Julia. "You've had a loss, and I feel you have been dealing with it well, armed with a good attitude. Someday, and I hope soon, things will change for the better. You'll find that person who can bring you joy and with whom you can be happy. You are not ready for a relationship, and neither am I. If both of us were, I'm sure we'd be very compatible. In the meanwhile, we can still be friends.''

Ralph agreed. As she left, they clasped hands in a gesture of friendship.

CHAPTER FOURTEEN

Ralph Steele was sitting in the waiting room of Dr. Allan Brown, the neurosurgeon who had performed his surgery three weeks previously. He was to remove the stitches from the incision, and give Ralph a final checkup.

He sat in an upholstered chair, looking at a current issue of Newsweek. His mind began to wander: he kept thinking of the distasteful episode with Julia. Yes, he did want a relationship. He would like to continue on with a person just as he had left off with Rosalie. But the rules had changed. People like Julia wanted friendship, rather than commitment in a relationship that would provide the necessary ingredient of companionship. Yes, he still would be friends, but he would continue to search for that right person. Surely, there had to be someone who shared the same ideals and looked upon a relationship as one primarily of companionship.

"Mr. Steele, the doctor will see you now," said the nurse standing in the doorway, holding a thick folder. As he got up from his chair, the nurse asked him to follow her to an examination room. Once inside she assured him, "I'll only be a few minutes and then Dr. Brown will be with you."

"Thank you," he replied as he sat on a stool.

Within minutes the doctor appeared, followed by a nurse carrying a tray of surgical scissors and medical supplies.

"Good morning, Mr. Steele. Nice to see you," he greeted.

"Well it's nice to see you in this environment, rather than the time we met for surgery," Ralph replied.

Dr. Brown laughed and said, "All my patients say the same thing. You're here after the fact. Now let's take the bandages off and see what this looks like." He was pleased with what he saw, and in a methodical manner removed the stitches, saying, "Well, that was painless, wasn't it?"

Ralph asked whether they had gotten all of the cancer, since the results of the second opinion were not back.

"Based on my own experience with this surgical procedure, which I have performed many times over the years, my observation is that at most it was a low-grade tumor. When you see Dr. Pare, he may recommend several radiation treatments to take care of any of the tentacles that could not be removed during surgery. Otherwise, you're doing fine, and that hair is really growing back quickly. We'll leave the bandages off, since you've healed fine," Dr. Brown told him.

When he returned home, a package from the college was in the rack of the mail box. It was from Violet. He took it inside, opened the flap, and removed the contents. The proposal that Violet had arranged to pick up had been typed, so he went inside and sat at the kitchen table to proofread it. Any additions or deletions that he would want to make would be easy for Violet to correct, since she put everything on the word processor in her office.

Ralph looked at the calendar and the date for him to see Dr. Pare was the following day. He hoped that the results of the other pathologist's report was back from the laboratory.

"Ralph, I'm afraid I have some bad news. You're in the big time now," Dr. Pare announced when he arrived for his checkup the next day. "The report came back and you have lymphoma cancer. If we don't treat it immediately you may have as little as eight months to live."

Ralph was shocked, even though there had been a possibility of cancer. He asked, "What do you recommend?"

The doctor responded, "Dr. Alex Jenson, who is across the hall from this office, is available to begin treatment on you so we can lick this thing. If you wish, I'll have Nancy, my nurse, call over and let him know you'll be coming over."

"It's okay with me," replied Ralph.

Dr. Pare nodded and then left the room. In several minutes he returned and said, "It's all arranged. Dr. Jenson is located in Suite 310. You can't miss it." With that, Ralph left and walked to Dr. Jenson's office, feeling like a ton of bricks had hit him. He introduced himself to the receptionist in a shaky voice. She motioned for him to follow her as she led him to an examination room.

Shortly afterwards, Doctor Jenson appeared and said, "Well, we have a chair open, so we'll get you started on intravenous chemotherapy."

"But I thought I would be treated with radiation," Ralph replied in surprise.

"No, no, we can't treat you with radiation, especially when the cancer is throughout your whole body," he explained.

"But, what about all of the tests that I took before the operation?" Ralph asked, terrified. "Other than the tumor which showed up in the MRI and was removed in surgery, the rest of the tests were good, or so I was led to believe."

"What tests?" asked the doctor.

"Let's stop right here. If you don't know about the tests that I took prior to surgery, then you probably haven't looked at them. How in the devil can you treat me!" Ralph fumed.

"You obviously are not willing to cooperate. Do you want another opinion?" asked the doctor.

"Hell, yes," Ralph replied angrily.

"Any place in particular?" he asked.

Ralph was furious and upset by what was happening. Recalling the conflicting reports of two pathologists, and what

Dr. Brown, his neurosurgeon, had told him, he lashed back, "If I'm in the big time now, then I want to go where the big-timers are, up north to the Tri-County Medical Clinic."

"Very well. Then I'll arrange an appointment for you, since you are very uncooperative," Dr. Jenson said in return.

As Ralph was leaving the office, the nurse at the reception desk said, "Mr. Steele, we'll call you and give you the information on the appointment at the Tri-County Medical Clinic as soon as the arrangements are made."

"Thank you," he replied.

As soon as arrangements were made, he flew north to the Medical Clinic, taking with him all of the results of the tests he had taken, including the two pathology reports. His attending physician at the clinic was Dr. John Dobbs, one of the leading cancer specialists in the country. Ralph was impressed by his efficiency and especially the kindness of his manner.

"Mr. Steele, we've scheduled some tests for you. First, an MRI, an EEG, EKG, and then some blood work. You'll have to stay overnight and tomorrow a neurologist, a neurosurgeon, and possibly a specialist of infectious diseases will take a look at you. Then we'll all get together and determine what treatment will be best for you. By late tomorrow, I should have some answers for you. Darlene, my nurse, will give you the time of your tests and appointments, including your return visit tomorrow," Dr. Dobbs informed him.

Things moved so quickly that he did not realize it was almost noon. He grabbed a sandwich and a glass of orange juice in the cafeteria and sat down to eat. That evening, he walked to his motel, went to his room, and laid down on his bed. He thought of the possibility of having to undergo the intravenous treatment. He would rather die than go through chemotherapy.

He fell asleep and when he awoke, it was morning. He looked at his watch and discovered he was late. He quickly showered, shaved and changed into clean clothes, then went to the motel lobby where a continental breakfast was served. It was too late to walk, so he took advantage of the shuttle bus that had just arrived to take people to the clinic. He met with his appointments that morning and everything the doctors were saying seemed positive.

At three o'clock an appointment was scheduled with Dr. Dobbs. He sat in a chair reading a magazine, waiting for the nurse at the reception desk to call out his name. It was getting beyond the appointment time, and he was getting nervous. Finally, she called, "Mr. Steele." A nurse with his folder stood by the side of the desk and smiled, saying, "Mr. Steele, come with me."

It seemed like an eternity for Ralph as he waited in one of the examining rooms. Suddenly the door burst open and there stood Dr. Dobbs with a smile on his face.

He sat at his desk and began to look over the contents of the folder. Then he turned to Ralph and said, "Mr. Steele, we have checked over your tests: those you took yesterday and those you had taken before. Our conclusion is — you do not have cancer." As Ralph sighed in relief, he continued, "We will want to see you in six months in order for us to monitor any new developments. My nurse will send you a letter when that time comes. Any questions?"

Ralph stared at the floor, tears dropping from his eyes to the floor like large rain drops, and he asked, "You mean, I do not have cancer?"

"That's right, all of it was successfully removed."

"Thank God," he said, wiping his eyes with his hankerchief. "I want to thank you, doctor, and all of the staff here at the clinic. I feel relieved. Thanks again," he said as he rose from his chair and shook Dr. Dobb's hand, placing his left arm on his shoulder.

On the flight back, Ralph felt as though a ton of bricks had been taken off his shoulders. He felt great. He wanted to begin a new life. Start over.

CHAPTER FIFTEEN

It was Wednesday, and he was home and anxious to do something. He remembered that Julia had said there was dancing at the Calumet Club on Wednesday and Thursday nights, so he seriously considered going.

As he was dressing, hc looked in the mirror and noticed that his hair had grown back. It was short, but he was able to brush it so that he could partially cover the scar on the right side of his head.

Before he left, he checked the telephone book for the address of the Calumet Club and then looked at an area road map to see where the club was located. He planned to eat at a fast-food restaurant on the way to Clarion, so he didn't have to take time to fix anything at home.

When he arrived at the Club a short time before eight, he was surprised that a Lingerie Show was taking place. He asked one of the waitresses if there was dancing that night and she replied, "Yes sir, but it doesn't start until nine. Why don't you sit down and enjoy the show?" She nudged him, saying,

"Maybe you'll see something the girls are wearing that you may want for the missus."

He didn't respond but followed her to a table that was located farthest from the dance floor, and in a corner of the room. A woman using a microphone was standing in the middle of the dance floor. Once seated, he saw models all wearing various fashions of lingerie walking down a makeshift runway. The woman at the microphone described what each model was wearing, and of course the price of the apparel. Then the models would make their way amongst the tables, stopping at each one, shimmering in silks and satins, making a pitch to the men sitting at the table to purchase the apparel. After the waitress had taken Ralph's order for a diet cola, the models approached his table. The models were very pleasant, but grew bold in their approach.

One of them went through her routine, explaining the garment to him. She was a woman in her thirties who appeared very cool, classy, and collected, and she enjoyed showing her chic, neat shape. She was wearing a knee-length robe that tied at the waist, turning gracefully to one side and then the other. She untied the robe, exposing a "V"-shaped lace thong-back teddy. She then asked, "Wouldn't you like to buy this for your wife?" When he did not respond, she said, "If she wore this, you'd sure get the hots."

Then she turned, raised the lace robe to her waist and moved in a sexual rhythm. She turned to him and said, "Now you'd like a little of this — wouldn't you?" She continued to the next table and another model took her place. This show continued until he observed the disc jockey moving his equipment into the room and beginning to set it up near the dance floor. He noticed that several women were coming in. It was nine o'clock, and the woman at the mike and the models began packing some suitcases and carrying them off the floor. He ordered another diet cola and sat at his corner table waiting for the dance to start. He became a little apprehensive when he realized that he was in a lounge and obviously this was not necessarily a singles dance. But since he was here he would wait and find out.

The music started and people began to dance. However, the men were asking women to dance. This scared him, but maybe he would get the courage to ask someone to dance.

He was on his third cola as he sat and continued to watch the couples as they danced or talked at tables.

"There you are!" a voice startled him from behind.

He looked up and saw the model who had been dressed in the fancy lace robe and who had talked to him about the "hots."

"May I join you?" she asked.

"Yes," he answered.

"I'll bet you don't remember me," she said to him, turning her head with a smile in her eyes.

"You're one of the models," he flatly replied.

"Which one?" she asked with a devilish look on her face.

He began to describe what she had modeled and she nodded her head in approval. "So, you do remember," she said.

The waitress approached the table and asked if she could help them. The young woman replied, "A glass of white wine, please." Ralph nodded no, and the waitress turned and left the table.

"I'm sorry," apologized the woman. "My name is Melissa Monroe, and I model for the Marx Agency here in Clarion."

"And my name is Ralph Steele," he said. "I'm the dean of the business and technical college which is located in Vernon Heights."

"Oh, gee, a big guy!" she replied.

He thought that maybe it was wrong to tell her who he was, but he wasn't going to hide anything. The waitress brought the wine to the table and turned to Ralph and said, "That'll be two dollars please." He reached into his wallet and gave her a five dollar bill. She laid the change on the table.

"Thanks," said Melissa.

Ralph nodded and smiled at her. As she sipped the wine, he noticed she was an attractive young woman. Her face was almost heart-shaped with a small upturned nose and a gently dimpled chin. She had raven-black hair drawn back and tied

67

with a silver clasp. Her eyes were dark, and she wore bright red lipstick on her full, sensuous lips. After having had the opportunity of observing her marvelous body, the desire to hold her close in his arms became overwhelming.

As the music slowed, he asked, "Would you have this dance with me?" They got up from the table and moved toward the dance floor. She stood there, waiting for him to embrace her. Together they shared a very sexy dance. She moved close into him and he could feel her breasts on his chest. He noticed several couples dancing where the man had his hands on the woman's derriere. He became impulsive and slowly lowered his arms around her. She responded by wrapping her arms around his back, and they danced as one. After the music stopped, they both longed for another dance. Again the music was soft and slow. He enjoyed every sensation that came over him and felt a tremendous desire to have this woman for his own. The music stopped, and they were still entwined in each other's arms, when a tall, handsome man came between them and said, "Melissa, you promised me a dance. How about the next one coming up?"

She looked at Ralph and he said, "It's all right. Go ahead."

Ralph went back to the table and found two couples sitting there. He looked around and decided to go up and stand by the bar. Several dance numbers were played and he did not see Melissa anywhere. He motioned to the waitress and asked about Melissa. "Have you seen the gal I was with earlier?" he asked.

"Oh, that dark-haired woman. Yeah, I saw her leave with some tall, good-looking guy," she answered.

Ralph decided that he had had enough for the night. Obviously, she had found the young man who cut in to dance with her more appealing than him. Yet, he would never forget the sensation that came over him when he danced with her. There would be more opportunities. He just had to be patient.

The next morning, Ralph decided to go to the office and give his edited copy of the proposal to Violet rather than call her on the telephone. He was feeling well enough, and since he had been dancing the night before, felt guilty that he was ignoring his responsibilities as dean.

Violet welcomed him as he came in the door. "Good morning, Mr. Steele, you're looking good."

"Thank you, Violet. I'd like to look over the mail, check on any memos that have come, and talk with Mr. Sims. To be honest, Violet, I'm just plain bored at home," he confessed, "so I'll stay for just a little while, then go home and rest as the doctors have instructed me to do."

He went into his office and found the mail that Violet had neatly placed on his desk. Most of it he considered to be junk mail since many vendors would use a computerized letter directed at the college or to him, pitching their product or special service as a first or exclusive offer. Of course, there was a price involved. As he was throwing most of this promotional mail into the wastebasket, Curtis Sims walked into his office.

"Hey, ol' buddy, Violet said you were in the building and you wanted to see me," he said.

"Yes, Curtis, have a seat," Ralph replied, motioning to a chair directly in front of his desk.

"You're looking good," Curtis said.

"I'm sorry that Maureen and I didn't get up to see you, Ralph, but there never seemed to be any time for us to make the trip to Clarion," he explained.

Ralph did not show his inner feelings. Nor would he confront him with what Violet had said about a visit Curtis made shortly after he was released to his room. Ralph looked down at the top of his desk and said, "Well, things happen sometimes and we can't do what we'd like. I'm interested in how things went, how the staff reacted, and anything else you feel I need to know."

Curtis appeared to be searching for words, but began, "Everything went smoothly, but there was one reaction from the staff I think you should know about."

"What's that Curtis?" he asked.

"Well, there's confusion amongst the staff."

69

Ralph began to frown, but let Curtis continue. "They feel there's a power struggle going on between the two of us. I don't know how it started, but I've heard some talk about your ability to continue after having brain surgery."

"Well, Curtis, you understand that any power you want to talk about rests in this office. Until the trustees remove me from this office, or I decide to leave, there is no power for you to struggle for. Is that clear?" he shot back.

"Well, I guess I'll go back to my office, Ralph. See you later." Curtis got up from the chair and began to leave.

"Before you leave, Curtis, I should tell you that I'm here for just a few hours. I plan on going home soon. The doctor wants me to take it easy for a month. I expect you to call me there if any problems arise," Ralph said.

"Gotcha," replied Curtis, jabbing his thumbs up.

After Curtis left, Ralph finished opening the mail. Before he left to go home, he asked Violet to send copies of his proposal to all of the trustees and members of the staff.

CHAPTER SIXTEEN

Ralph sat at the kitchen table looking out the window thinking about the conversation he had with Curtis Sims. He didn't quite understand why Curtis would mention to him that he and Maureen were sorry about not visiting him in the hospital when Curtis had told Violet that he had been there when he was brought back from intensive care. And this talk about a power struggle. Curtis didn't offer that he tried to ward off any such talk among the staff. Sometimes a person who is self serving and ambitious can be very dangerous in an organization because they do seek power. Did Curtis fit the mold, and if so was he strong enough in the college politics to succeed?

Ralph decided that it would be best if he took his mind off of what intentions Curtis had, but be careful of his actions. He decided to return to the Calumet Club in order to keep his mind off of Curtis' remarks. He hoped that there wouldn't be any lingerie show going on since he wanted to dance and perhaps have some conversation with some ladies who would be there.

As he entered the club, the same waitress who had waited on him the night before greeted him asking, "Hello sir, would you like a table?"

"Yes, that would be fine," he replied.

"The same one as last night okay?" she asked, winking.

"I have no preference," he replied.

She led him to the same table he had the night before and as he began to sit down, she asked, "Can I get you a drink?"

He replied, "Yes, a diet cola."

She turned and left for the bar. He began to look around and observed that the room had very few people in it. When the waitress returned with his drink, he remarked that there were very few people present. As she set his drink on the table, she commented, "It's too early. The music usually starts around nine and within an hour, the place is packed." She reached for the ten dollar bill that he put down, and replaced it with eight dollars and fifty cents change. He sipped on his drink and sank back into the captain's chair he was sitting on.

As he sat with his head tilted back and his eyes closed, he felt a tap on his shoulder.

"Hey, do you remember me?" someone whispered softly into his ear. He turned to see a woman smiling down at him.

"Don't you remember — last night. I was in the show, and you sat here at this same table," she said disappointedly.

She was a woman with a very slim body wearing a tight-fitting flamboyant yellow dress.

"Come, sit down," he said pushing one of the captain's chairs out so she could move into position to sit down.

"My name is Sheila Sells, and I work for the same agency that Melissa works for," she replied, then added, "Melissa is the gal you were dancing with last night. You remember, don't you?"

"And my name is Ralph Steele," he answered.

"Nice to meet you," she said smiling.

"Likewise," he nodded.

He motioned for the waitress as he asked her what she wanted to drink.

"I'll have a diet cola," she replied.

When the waitress came, he ordered the drinks.

He noticed that her face was heart shaped with a straight nose. The make-up she used accentuated her hazel eyes with long lashes and the frosted lipstick on her small lips. She had a black beauty mark on her cheek.

"Where's Melissa tonight?" he asked.

"Oh, she's probably at one of those bars where she can meet men. She's still looking for Mr. Right and having a hard time finding him," she replied.

She saw the frown come over his face and continued, "She's desperate to have a baby and has been unable to find a man suited to her tastes." She paused and added, "I think it's sad. Take me for instance. I was married at seventeen and divorced when I was twenty-five. I raised two kids without any help from my ex. Thank God my kids are grown and I have some space again."

"How old are your children?" he asked.

"My daughter is twenty-four and has two kids, both boys, and my son is twenty-two and going to school out on the West Coast," she answered.

"What about you, any kids?" she asked with a crooked smile.

Ralph replied, "I have four, two boys and two girls. They're all grown up and have families of their own."

"Any wife?"

"No. She passed away six months ago."

The drinks arrived at the table and as the waitress was setting them down she said, "The music's gonna start." Then added, "The disc jockey was late and everyone is a little upset. They wanna dance, I guess."

As they began to sip at their drinks, she said, "Ralph, come over and sit close to me."

He moved one of the captain's chairs that was between them out of the way and scooted his chair close to hers.

The music started and it was loud and fast.

"Oh, this is going to be disco night," said Sheila.

73

A look of disappointment grew over Ralph's face as he said, "I don't enjoy that jumping up and down dancing."

"I don't either, Ralph," she replied, and added, "Let's just sit here and hold hands and watch the people dance."

They held hands under the table. She put her head on his shoulder and the aroma of the perfume in her hair aroused him. As she turned to look into his eyes, her body drew closer to him and she kissed him.

"Ralph honey, we can go to my place and play some of my tapes with slow dance music, and we can really enjoy one another," she suggested.

"Sure, darling," he said as his lips came down on hers passionately.

"Excuse me, there's a call for a Sheila Sells," announced the waitress as she stood at the table opposite them.

"Who is it?" Sheila asked.

"The bartender over at the Cavalier Club. Something about a Melissa Monroe," she replied.

"Oh my, she's in trouble again. I better go Ralph. See you," she said getting up from the table to leave. "I hope we can get together sometime soon, and get to become better acquainted," she added. As she left the Calumet Club, a tall dark handsome young man came out from one of the pay phone booths and watched her as she drove away. He then left the club.

In the lobby of the Hotel Regency, two men were talking. One was an elderly man dressed in a black suit with a gray vest, matching the spats that partially covered his well polished black shoes. His hair was almost pure white in color and combed neatly, making him look distinguished. The other man was tall and handsome with dark wavy hair. He wore a navy blue suit.

"Michael, you've asked me to come. What is it that is troubling you?" the elderly man asked.

"Angel Gordian, as the leader of our legion of guardian angels, my concern is with Ralph Steele. He is running completely out of control," replied the tall handsome young man.

"And how can I be of help?"

"In his desire to find companionship and true love, he has fallen into the ways of the fast singles life. I have had to rescue him on several occasions from these sinful ways. A pattern is developing that will lead him into a life of sin. If only I could be assigned one of our beautiful angels to assist me in distracting him away from the transgressions of these women who seem to want to exploit him, I believe that we can be successful in preventing another soul from falling to the wiles and wickedness of Satan."

"I have such an angel in mind, Michael. Her name is Angelica, and she would be capable of such an assignment."

"Thank you Gordian, I am happy that you would see the predicament that I am in and help me."

"I will get in touch with you as soon as arrangements are made."

When the men ended their conversation, they each went their way.

CHAPTER SEVENTEEN

Ralph was disappointed that each time he met a woman who could give him companionship, something always turned up. In the case with Melissa, she evidently was attracted to the tall good-looking young man. And in Sheila's case, she was more concerned with helping her friend than being with him. The telephone rang and when he answered, Violet was on the other end.

"Mr. Steele, John Appling and Mark Phillips have called and want to see you today. They want to know if it's possible to set up an appointment."

"Set something up for two o'clock, Violet, and I'll be there." Ralph wondered what their concerns were since they seldom came to his office.

At two o'clock he met them in his office. John Appling was an accountant in Vernon Heights, and Mark Phillips had an agricultural background and was in the farm implement business as a salesman. As they entered his office, Ralph met them at the door and greeted them, inviting them to sit down.

He walked back to his chair, sat down, and leaning back, said, "Gentlemen, what do I owe the pleasure of this visit?"

John Appling began by saying, "We both received a copy of your proposal and have some questions for you."

"And what might those questions be?" Ralph asked.

John replied, "First of all, I don't like the involvement of the industrial council. What right do they have making recommendations? After all, we on the board of trustees are the decision-makers."

"And we don't like you going behind our backs and getting support from the business people so we will have no choice but to implement your plan," added Mark Phillips sternly.

"Why would you think that?" Ralph asked.

"Because they had known about the proposal much earlier than us. We finally received a copy of it just the other day," he retorted.

"Well, what are the specifics which you are in disagreement with?" asked Ralph in return.

"Well," John Appling answered, "Why should we retrain employees when business has plenty of money and should do that themselves? Besides, there are all kinds of government programs to take care of laid-off employees."

Mark Phillips expressed his concern that the staff was not involved in the development of the plan, saying, "the instructors don't like the idea of having to develop performance objectives. They feel it's too much of a load for the good it will do."

John Appling continued, "It is not for us to approve a plan which states that we only want to attract those young people who have a potential of becoming productive employees. As I said earlier, business has the money to recruit their own future employees to be productive workers for them. Your whole plan is like a sieve that won't hold water. As a result, the trustees won't approve it."

"Gentlemen, I can see that you do not have any understanding of the role both public and private business and technical education facilities play in the retention of jobs for the

77

economy of the community. The department of development has set aside funds to assist business and industry with training, so there will not be any financial burden on the college. In order to qualify to provide this training, we must have a plan, our courses must be brought up to date in order to meet the changing technology that we face today, or we will only be a place for students to pass through and not obtain the skills required to obtain gainful employment."

"This proposal is still too much, too fast," replied Mark Phillips.

"I hope you understand that I have worked on this proposal at the request of the trustees even though I am dealing with personal tragedy and health problems. The communication between us could have been better, but under the circumstances, I could not help it. I am sorry if I have offended you."

"Ralph," said John Appling, "Quit wallowing in self-pity."

Ralph only smiled and said, "I'm sure that we can discuss these issues in the future."

John Appling suggested, "Ralph, why don't you send every trustee an explanation of each point in your proposal. It may clear up any misunderstanding of what you're trying to do."

"One last thing, Ralph . . . why haven't you given Curtis Sims more responsibility, especially in helping you with this proposal? He's a good man," Mark Phillips added.

"It's time to go," said John, looking at his watch. "I guess we've said our piece. We appreciate your time." The two left the office as Ralph grappled with the disappointment he was feeling from the opposition of two of the five trustees.

CHAPTER EIGHTEEN

Ralph was stunned by this latest turn of events. He tried to control himself, but he could not hold back the hurt and the anger. He did not appreciate the remark about self-pity. He believed that even though his life was topsy-turvy and his emotions were on a roller coaster, he was going to fight for a life of happiness.

He remembered his loneliness after Rosalie's death, and the major surgery he had undergone with the threat of cancer devastating his will to live. Now the possible undermining of his proposal by the two trustees' unyielding position angered him.

Throughout all these ordeals his faith in God had grown, and he continued to pray to Him in a steadfast manner.

The mention of Curtis Sims by the trustees had startled him. Could he trust him? He recalled the lie Curtis had made about having visited at the hospital and his comment regarding a power struggle between them. During his stay in the hospital, Curtis had been handling some of his duties and would have had some contact with the trustees. He also covered for him at one of the meetings of the business council, so he could have obtained first-hand the council's responses to his training proposal.

It was Saturday, so Ralph decided to sleep in, only to be awakened by the ring of the telephone. When he answered it, the male voice at the other end said, "Hello, is this Ralph Steele?"

"Yes, may I help you?"

"This is George Stevens from the support group. Do you remember me?"

"Sure," Ralph replied, "You're the World War II vet."

"I didn't make it to the singles dance that the rest of the support group went to. I'd like to go this Sunday night but I don't want to go alone. Are you free to go with me?"

Ralph thought for a moment, then replied, "Sure, I'll go. Between the two of us, we might learn to have a good time!"

"What time do you want me to pick you up?" he asked eagerly.

"Around seven o'clock? That'll give us plenty of time to get there by eight o'clock."

"Okay, see you then," said George.

CHAPTER NINETEEN

Ralph sat in a chair in the family room waiting for George Stevens to come and pick him up. He wasn't really excited about going to the singles dance, but he wanted to oblige George. Perhaps going out would take his mind off the trouble that seemed to be brewing at the college. First thing on Monday morning he thought it would be a good move to call Miles Weller and have lunch. Then he could find out what Miles thought, since he was not only a good businessman but a friend as well.

A car pulled into the driveway and Ralph heard the horn. As he looked out the window, he saw a late model Cadillac in the driveway with George Stevens sitting behind the wheel. He waved and then went out the door, locking it behind him.

As Ralph approached the car he said, "Hi George." George reached over and opened the passenger door for him. "Had a little trouble finding your place, but I got here."

On the way to Clarion, George told him how he had decided at the last minute not to go to the singles dance with the support group. "I guess I just wasn't ready," he explained.

"You don't have to offer explanations. You have to feel right when you do something. I'm happy to be of help by going with you," Ralph replied.

"Thanks, I'm glad to hear that. I didn't want to be a bother." George talked of the extreme loneliness he was feeling and thought that perhaps Jim Martin was right, socializing at singles dances might help.

"You can be sure there's no medicine to cure loneliness," replied Ralph.

George pulled into the parking lot of the Clarion Hotel at eight o'clock sharp. As they left the car and walked to the lobby of the hotel, Ralph said, "We'll have to register to get into the dance."

Inside the lobby, Ralph motioned for George to follow him. The two went down the hallway and to the registration tables for the dance. Once George completed filling out the information cards, they paid and went inside.

Ralph was feeling confident and tried to calm George who seemed to be very nervous. He remembered his feelings the first time he had come.

"Let's sit over here at this table," Ralph suggested. It was the same round table where he had sat before. He pointed out the cash bars at each end of the room, but George didn't appear interested. Instead, he was looking over the group of people, especially the women.

Ralph went to the bar and ordered a small diet cola. He handed the waitress a dollar bill in exchange for the drink, and went back to the table. He looked up and saw that George was dancing. That leg of his sure didn't seem to bother him, he thought. When the dance ended, he came to the table, followed by the woman he was dancing with. It so happened that she was sitting at the same table as they were, so Ralph assumed they had met while he was getting his drink. The two sat down, leaving an empty chair between George and him. He thought that George hadn't wasted any time since he was deeply engrossed in conversation with the woman. Ralph looked away, sipping at his drink and watching the people as they moved about waiting for the next dance to begin.

It was then that he noticed a very attractive woman sitting in the chair next to him. He turned and their eyes met. He said hello and she returned the greeting.

"Would you like something to drink?" he asked.

She nodded and said, "Cola would be fine."

He went for a drink and returned to the table saying, "There you are," as he placed the drink down on the table. As he was sitting down he said to her, "My name is Ralph Steele. What's yours?"

"Angelica," she replied, "Angelica Baron."

She had a gentle smile on her lips as she spoke. Her face was oval with a dainty nose. Her soft blue eyes had long lashes, and her radiant smile showed the delightful dimples in her cheeks and chin. Layers of curled golden locks of hair flowed softly to her shoulders, smelling like honeysuckle.

"Do you dance Ralph?" she asked.

"Yes, but I'm no Fred Astaire!" he said, observing the dance floor where couples were dancing to a waltz.

When the music started for the next dance, she asked, "Ralph, if you dance, will you dance with me?"

"I'll be glad to dance with you, Angelica," he replied, as he stood up and turned to her, helping her get out from her chair. She was a startling beauty, of medium height and gracefully slender. When they reached the dance floor, he modestly embraced her as they danced to slow, romantic music. When it was over he said to her, "Angelica, may I have the next dance?"

"Yes, you may," she replied.

They danced a number of times, only returning to the table when the disc jockey would play fast numbers. "As they were sitting down, George said, "I'd like you to meet Blanche," as he put his arm around her.

Ralph in turn introduced them to Angelica. They exchanged greetings. Then there was an announcement that the last dance of the evening was about to begin. Ralph and Angelica looked at one another and smiled as they got up and went to the dance floor. After the dance, George asked Ralph, "Are you planning on taking Angelica home?'' Ralph looked at her blue eyes twinkle as she nodded yes. ''That will be fine with us,'' he replied.

As they were driving home, Ralph was surprised to learn that Angelica lived in an apartment on the outskirts of town, and worked in a preschool child care facility nearby. She believed that her work in education was very rewarding and seemed pleased to know that he was involved in preparing people for work. As she cuddled closer to him, the fragrance of the honeysuckle was breathtaking. He placed his arm around her and reaching down, kissed her forehead tenderly. She put her head on his shoulder and he wrapped his arms closer around her.

Then George turned around and asked, ''Which way to your house, Angelica?'' he asked. She rose up in the seat and began to give him directions. When he reached the street where she lived, she said, ''It's the fourth building on the left.'' There were a number of small apartment dwellings and she lived in one of the efficiencies. Ralph walked her to the door.

''Thanks for a wonderful evening,'' she said.

''The pleasure was all mine, I thank you.''

He reached down and kissed her on the forehead. She in return kissed him on the cheek. ''Good night,'' she said as she entered her apartment.

''Good night,'' he replied as he turned and walked to the car and got in.

The next morning Ralph called Miles Weller and asked him if he could stop by his office.

''Sure, Ralph, what time?'' he asked.

''After lunch, say around one o'clock,'' he replied. The telephone rang and it was Rose Matthews. She sounded excited. ''Ralph, I have great news for you. We have a buyer for your house and at the asking price.''

''That's great news. What do we do now?'' he asked.

''If you're going to be there for a while, I'll drop by and have you sign to accept their offer. They have financing, so we'll be able to close in four to six weeks,'' she answered.

"I'll be here until lunch, so I'll look forward to seeing you," he said. He told Violet that Rose Matthews would be coming by shortly and Miles Weller had an appointment with him after lunch. Minutes later, Rose came through the door carrying a file folder. She explained the offer to purchase and asked him to sign. After he signed the agreement, he said, "Rose, I'll be needing an apartment to move into. Since you've done such an excellent job of selling the house, I'm sure you'll find an apartment for me."

"I'll start working on it right away," she replied.

"I'll be waiting to hear from you," he said as she left. During lunch Ralph kept thinking about Angelica. She was beautiful and so graceful as she moved. He had noticed her hands were small and her fingers petite, and the radiant smile that she wore was cheerful. He wondered if he would ever see her again. When he returned to the office, he looked in the telephone book to see if she was listed, and found she was not. He heard Miles Weller come in so he went to greet him.

"Thanks for coming over Miles," he said.

They both sat at the conference table and before Ralph could say anything, Miles spoke up. "Ralph, I know something is bothering you. I could tell from the tone of your voice."

"Miles, you're right, something is bothering me. Yesterday, John Appling and Mark Phillips stopped in and expressed dissatisfaction with the proposal I developed. It seems to me that they have lost confidence in me."

"What did they say?"

"They don't like the idea of having programs available for the business community for retraining their employees to meet the new technology, nor do they like the idea of having programs for laid-off employees. They feel that business has money to do those things and so does the government. They forget that there is funding available through the state department of development for these programs.

"But the kicker is that they are listening to the staff whine about having to improve their courses with performance based objectives. They resent allowing the industrial council which I've been working with to have any input on this."

"Ralph, don't let those two get under your skin. You still have the support of the rest of us. Frankly, it's a good proposal, so don't worry," Miles said in a reassuring way.

"Thanks for coming over Miles and hearing me out."

"That's what friends are for," replied Miles as he got up to leave. "No more talk about lack of confidence."

As he was driving home he felt more at ease knowing that the chairmen of the trustees, Miles Weller, who was also a friend, as well as the other trustees had confidence in him.

As he pulled into his driveway, he noticed a young woman standing in front of his house, leaning against a bicycle. She was holding something in her hand. When he got closer, he was surprised and delighted to see that it was Angelica. As he stopped the car and got out she waved, saying, "Hi! I was wondering if you'd ever get here. I brought something for you." She held out the package and said, "I baked some brownies for you."

Ralph said with a smile, "Thank you very much. It's so nice to see you." She looked so beautiful standing there with her golden hair glistening in the sun.

"Won't you come in? I'll make a pot of coffee, and we can have a brownie and a cup of coffee together," he suggested.

"No, I must go," she replied as she handed him the brownies.

"Are you sure you won't change your mind?" he asked.

"No, I can't stay. I must go home. Goodbye," she said as she straddled the bicycle and started to peddle. She biked slowly down the driveway and before turning onto the street, waved and moved quickly out of sight.

CHAPTER TWENTY

The next day he saw Angelica as she rode her bicycle down the street that led to Cove Valley State Park. Bicycle and nature trails were one of the highlights of the area. There was also a lake with a beach and boat ramps for fishermen that attracted people to the park. Several of the local garden clubs had been given space to plant flower gardens along the trails. He followed her until he was able to get her attention by honking the horn of his car.

She stopped and with her radiant smile said, "It's you," wiping her brow with her forearm.

"Yes," he replied. "I saw you riding your bicycle and thought I'd stop you to see if you'll have dinner with me tonight."

She thought for a moment and said, "I'd like to see the flowers and plants in the gardens along the trails first, and after that I can give you an answer." She asked him to join her, and he replied, "Okay, but it's still a ways down the road. Let's put your bicycle in the trunk of my car and we can ride there together." She nodded her assent. After he placed the bicycle in the trunk and held it in place with a cord, they rode off to the park.

They walked down the paths that were lined on each side with beautiful flowers and neatly trimmed evergreens. He had never been to the park, although he had heard so much about what the garden clubs had done. He marveled at the neatly placed flowers which blended in so well with the greenery of the plants, complementing the scheme of nature and leaving those seeing it awestruck.

Then they came to a grassy area where benches had been placed under flowering shade trees. She grabbed his hand and tugged at him, saying, "Let's sit down and rest for awhile." He followed her and they sat down. She looked around and admired all of the marvelous work that had such a beautiful plan. He thought that fall would soon be coming, followed by winter, which would change the appearance of the garden, revolving around the master plan God had created for the surroundings of earth.

As they started to walk again down a path that led to a lily patch, he turned to her and said, "You are so beautiful, Angelica, standing next to those lilies."

With a smile and that twinkle in her eyes, she said, "Ralph, it is so nice of you to say that. Thank you."

After he had taken her home, she agreed to go to dinner with him. "Great," he said, "I'll pick you up at six and we'll go to the Clarion Hotel. I understand that they have excellent food."

He returned home to get ready. Ralph had not felt this overpowering sense of rapturous delight for a long time. He was excited about his dinner date with Angelica. When the time came, he dressed, and went to pick her up. She looked gorgeous in a light blue dress, her hair of golden curled locks that fell softly to her shoulders. For the first time, he noticed the warmth of the gentle smile of her lips that were sensual.

Her voice was clear and sweet as she said, "I'll be right with you Ralph." He stood there and in a few minutes she reappeared saying, "I'm ready now."

As Ralph walked her to his car, and opened the door for her, he said, "Angelica, you look so beautiful, just like an angel."

"Thank you Ralph, you know it's the second time you said that to me today," she replied.

They were surprised to learn upon arriving at the Clarion Hotel that there was dancing later in the evening. After a dinner of lobster and steak, they sat at the table and talked, she of the beauty of the gardens in the park, and he of how he enjoyed her company and the joy of being with her.

This would be the beginning of a wonderful summer. They danced that night and many nights through the summer. There were picnics and strolls along the hiking trails in the park. They held each other close and kissed warmly and with affection.

Toward the end of the summer, he told her that he had something very important to tell her, but seemed reluctant to do so. Finally, he said as he kissed her, "Angelica, I must tell you that I love you. I know it's soon but if I get a good report from the clinic, I'll want to marry you. Do you love me?"

"I really don't know yet, it's too soon," she responded.

His appointment at the clinic was scheduled in September, and he was hoping for a good report. She could see the disappointment on his face so she said, "Ralph, let's wait a while longer." She wrapped her arms around him and tenderly planted a kiss on his lips.

It was one evening late in the summer that the angel Gordian payed a visit to Angelica. She did not expect him and asked him the purpose of his visit.

"Angelica, your mission here was to distract Ralph Steele, not fall in love with him," Gordian said firmly.

"I couldn't help it. He needed companionship, and we seemed to get along so well. I'm sorry," Angelica replied.

"You must understand, Angelica, that your change to a mortal being was for a limited period of time. That time is about to expire," Gordian explained.

"What does that mean?" she asked.

"Simply put, my dear, we will want you back by Christmas time," he responded. "You have a decision to make: either heavenly bliss, or a mortal life with Ralph Steele."

Angelica's eyes welled up with tears, and she began to sob.

"Please, my child," he advised, "You must pray and make this decision with your mind and heart, so you will enjoy happiness." He stretched both of his arms out and lay them on her shoulders and said, "Peace." He then left.

There was time to make this decision, she thought. It would be a difficult one, but she was determined to make it.

CHAPTER TWENTY-ONE

Rose Matthews called Ralph at the office and told him that she had obtained a two bedroom condominium located in a new subdivision between Vernon Heights and Clarion. She could meet him there later in the afternoon, and if interested would take care of a lease agreement. If he acted quickly, he could move in before the closing on his house in ten days. After seeing the condominium, he signed a two year lease agreement.

When he returned home that afternoon, he received a letter in the mail from the Tri-County Clinic notifying him of a return visit with Dr. Dobbs to monitor any possible new developments from his surgery.

That evening at dinner, he told Angelica of the condominium he was renting, and his need to prepare for a return to the Clinic.

"Things are really starting to jell," he told her, and added, "I'm going to move as soon as possible."

"I'm so glad for you. It will be a pleasant change for you, I'm sure," she replied.

"The house closing is in seven days, and a week later I have an appointment at the Clinic," and continued saying excitedly, "If I receive a good report, I'll come back and ask you to marry me."

"Oh," she said with a smile.

The time arrived for Ralph to leave for the Clinic. He had already moved into his new place after closing on the house. While he was at the Clinic, he became friends with Jonathan Owens. He had had surgery for prostate cancer and was in for a periodic checkup. Jonathan was president of the Acme Foundation, an organization supported by private donors that dealt primarily with research. He expressed an interest in Ralph, because of his extensive background in the world of work.

"Ralph, we always have room for people with your credentials. If you ever want to come to work for us, we'd sure take a hard look at you. Here's my card, call me if you decide," he said.

His organization was working on a project called Workplace 2000. Labor Department and Census Bureau statistics were two of the areas that were targets of research to project future job patterns.

"Jonathan, I support what you are doing, since many of the statistics you come up with are of benefit to those of us in the business and technical training area. I'm satisfied now, but you never know, I may be giving you a call," he said.

"Please, give me a call, even if it's just to visit on the phone," he said.

Ralph was called into Dr. Dobb's office, and as he left he said goodbye to his new acquaintance. The tests that he had taken were the same as before and Dr. Dobbs said, "Ralph, we see nothing that would indicate any possibility of cancer. Continue to take your anti-seizure medication and I believe you'll be okay."

Ralph was relieved, and as he boarded the plane to go home, he was anxious until it landed safely in Clarion. As he walked down the ramp, Angelica was there waiting for him.

She walked toward him and as they met and embraced, he reached down and kissed her.

"Is it good news?" she asked.

"The report was excellent. I do not have cancer," he said sighing in relief.

They walked down the concourse toward the main entrance where the telephones were to call a cab. As he was dialing for the operator, he looked at her and said, "I hope that when I ask the question, you will say yes."

She looked up at him and smiled with a twinkle in her eyes. They took a cab back to his place and dropped off the two small bags of luggage he had taken with him. He suggested they have dinner at the Stork and Nest Supper Club.

They sat at a table in a dimly lit room, the only light coming from a candle in the center of the table that glowed and occasionally flickered.

As they looked into each others' eyes he said, "Will you spend the rest of your life with me? I will with you."

And she answered him saying, "Ralph, I will because I love you so much."

They held hands and kissed across the table, vowing to bring each other joy and happiness. After dinner, they went back to the condominium and began to make plans. They would be married in a simple ceremony by Father Edwards at Saint Agnes Church. They would honeymoon by taking a cruise to the Caribbean. Ralph promised to make the arrangements.

———

They were married, and Father Edwards congratulated them and wished they would live a happy and rewarding life together. Angelica and Ralph packed their luggage and took the afternoon flight non-stop to Miami. They checked in with the cruiseline office and were cleared to board. As they walked up the steps to the platform that led to the ship, everyone would turn to have their picture taken. When Ralph and Angelica reached the top and turned to have their picture taken, Angelica smiled and waved softly to the two men at the bottom of the stairs, Gordian and Michael who also were smiling and waving.

Angel of love, my companion dear;
You have given me hope in a very sweet way,
Your tenderness has eased the perils of life,
Which has taken away my troubles and fear.

You are my angel, my comfort,
Who was there for me when I was in need,
Who has been a loving partner, and
Most of all my dearest companion indeed.